# MAKING THE MOST
## OF THE
# MEDIA

# MAKING THE MOST OF THE MEDIA

# MEDIA

*How to Profit from the Opportunities of Exposure*

## MICHAEL BARRATT

KOGAN PAGE

## YOURS TO HAVE AND TO HOLD
### BUT NOT TO COPY

The publication you are reading is protected by copyright law. This means that the publisher could take you and your employer to court and claim heavy legal damages if you make unauthorised photocopies from these pages. Photocopying copyright material without permission is no different from stealing a magazine from a newsagent, only it doesn't seem like theft.

The Copyright Licensing Agency (CLA) is an organisation which issues licences to bring photocopying within the law. It has designed licensing services to cover all kinds of special needs in business, education and government.

If you take photocopies from books, magazines and periodicals at work your employer should be licensed with CLA. Make sure you are protected by a photocopying licence.

The Copyright Licensing Agency Limited, 90 Tottenham Court Road, London, W1P 0LP. Tel: 0171 436 5931. Fax: 0171 436 3986.

First published in 1996

Apart from any fair dealing for the purposes of research or private study, or criticism or review, as permitted under the Copyright, Designs and Patents Act, 1988, this publication may only be reproduced, stored or transmitted, in any form or by any means, with the prior permission in writing of the publishers, or in the case of reprographic reproduction in accordance with the terms and licences issued by the CLA. Enquiries concerning reproduction outside those terms should be sent to the publishers at the undermentioned address:

Kogan Page Limited
120 Pentonville Road
London N1 9JN

© Michael Barratt, 1996

The right of Michael Barratt to be identified as author of this work has been asserted by him in accordance with the Copyright, Designs and Patents Act 1988.

**British Library Cataloguing in Publication Data**
A CIP record for this book is available from the British Library.

ISBN 0 7494 2037 5

Typeset by BookEns Ltd., Royston, Herts.
Printed and bound in Great Britain by Biddles Ltd,
Guildford and Kings Lynn

# Contents

*Foreword*   7

CHAPTER ONE
The power of the media ... the multi-million-pound yardstick ... and the thrill of it all   9

CHAPTER TWO
Accentuate the positive ... with a little help from your friend!   17

CHAPTER THREE
The most important skill of all ... the art of listening   25

CHAPTER FOUR
Born bilingual ... and the need for simple English   31

CHAPTER FIVE
The right royal way to influence but not manipulate ... and how to develop a relationship   37

CHAPTER SIX
Better the devil you know ... behind the scenes   43

CHAPTER SEVEN
Television ... the art of persuasion ... and projection   49

CHAPTER EIGHT
Radio ... the missing dimension ... and the need for colour   57

CHAPTER NINE
The press ... a question of ethics ... off-the-record dangers and opportunities   63

CHAPTER TEN
The professionals who aren't professional ... and the way to turn the tables   71

CHAPTER ELEVEN
Crisis! ... preparing for the worst   77

CHAPTER TWELVE
On your own ... forward with technology ... but back to basics   83

## MAKING THE MOST OF THE MEDIA

**CHAPTER THIRTEEN**
The inside job ... lessons of the revolution — 93

**CHAPTER FOURTEEN**
Do-it-yourself media promotion ... how to score now the goalposts have been moved — 101

**CHAPTER FIFTEEN**
The benefits of training ... and how to go shopping for the best package — 107

**CHAPTER SIXTEEN**
Practice session ... the 'easy' interview that can be difficult — 115

**CHAPTER SEVENTEEN**
More practice ... the 'difficult' interview that can be easy! — 123

**CHAPTER EIGHTEEN**
All together now ... the challenges of discussions and confrontations — 129

**CHAPTER NINETEEN**
The cosmetics ... putting the gloss on the right foundation — 135

**CHAPTER TWENTY**
The politician's way ... and some lessons for businesspeople — 141

**CHAPTER TWENTY-ONE**
Being prepared ... the morality of media training through other eyes — 147

**CHAPTER TWENTY-TWO**
In praise of brevity ... and the PR skills that aid communication — 151

**CHAPTER TWENTY-THREE**
Awards spell rewards ... how to get your stall out for pots of media gold — 157

**CHAPTER TWENTY-FOUR**
You're on your own ... the individual's guide to fame and fortune — 163

**CHAPTER TWENTY-FIVE**
Don't take my word for it ... listen to the other professionals! — 169

*Index* — *174*

# Foreword

If I live to be a hundred (the day after tomorrow) I will still be shy about giving advice.

There's still so much to learn. So how can I possibly teach?

And yet I have spent more than half a century in the media world – in newspapers, radio and television – so I suppose by now there's enough experience for me to share with others who want to exploit the opportunities on offer. Hence this book.

It is primarily for men and women in business who recognise the immense power of communication and who want to harness it profitably, but I'm also keen to convert some of the many doubters who fear rather than welcome exposure.

It's a brief book – because I preach brevity – but I hope it encompasses the key factors in 'getting the company message across'.

It may also help individuals in their personal development (and therefore in their careers).

There are a number of case histories recorded, because I have always believed in basing training on factual example rather than fantasy or hypothesis. I hope those mentioned will survive the repetition of their media experiences!

There are others who I hope have not suffered too painfully: all those audiences who have been the victims of my lifelong self-imposed discipline never to read a speech – explained in later chapters.

The victims of my training technique who have been put through the mill in often embarrassing fashion as I've tried to prepare them for the rigours of facing the media.

**MAKING THE MOST OF THE MEDIA**

My personal assistant, Margaret Ostler, who has had to fight the clock typing my scribbles in order to meet the publisher's deadline (why are we journalists incapable of getting down to productive work until some time past the eleventh hour?).

My family who have had to put up with my self-inflicted panic so near the twelfth hour ('I can't talk just now – got to finish the book'). It seems to be the done thing to dedicate a book, so this one's for them ...

My wife Dilys and our Jessica, Barnaby and Oliver. Love you!

CHAPTER ONE

• • • • • • • • • • • • • • • •

# The power of the media ... the multi-million-pound yardstick ... and the thrill of it all

My first job on a newspaper (apart from fetching the editor's tea) was writing the horoscope. I was 16. It was a simple task with easily-observed rules: avoid predictions that are precise enough to be proved wrong (so: 'Tuesday will be a good time to seek new friendships') and always give morally good advice ('Curb a tendency to lose your temper on Friday').

My introduction to radio came at the age of 24 and I began a weekly series of talks on politics for the Northern Nigerian Broadcasting Service. The Hausa and Fulani peoples of the region were about to achieve independence from their British colonial masters and the local District Officer felt that they could learn many lessons about the nature of Westminster-style democracy from an 'experienced' journalist like me.

As for television, I have John Profumo to thank for my venture into the dizzy world of BBC television's *Panorama* and other current affairs programmes. The War Minister's scandalous liaison with Christine Keeler had rocked Harold Macmillan's government and *Panorama* set out to examine the impact of the affair on the grass roots of the Tory party around the country. Their choice of a reporter to cover the Midlands was, unaccountably, me.

Indelible still is the memory of standing quaking in a Birmingham studio, waiting for the great Richard Dimbleby to 'hand over' to me from the London studio. Quite blank is the memory of actually delivering one minute's worth of memorised script – no autocue then – 'live' to an audience of millions.

Afterwards that Monday evening, the call came for me to meet another colossus of TV journalism, (now Sir) Paul Fox, *Panorama*'s editor. It was the beginning of a television career that meant my appearing on 'the box' almost nightly for many years to come.

During more than half a century now in the pursuit of professional excellence in all three branches of the media – the press, radio and television – I've learned a thing or two about the power of communication and the ways in which that power can be used or abused.

It's fashionable, I suppose, with some to take a snooty moral stance about those in commerce and industry who learn to practise media skills to their own advantage. I can't for the life of me understand this view and you certainly won't find it reflected in the following chapters. If you're proud of your business and conduct it with high standards of integrity and service, what on earth can be discreditable in promoting it with flair?

Indeed, I believe that most progressive media practitioners – the broadcasters and journalists – actually *welcome* the efforts businesspeople (yes, and even politicians!) make to improve their performances when being interviewed. In the studio or on location, I've always preferred the lucid, effective, quick-witted and persuasive interviewee to the hesitant, unconvincing, defensive one. As we shall see, the aim of the interviewer is not to reduce a 'victim' to a gibbering wreck, but to establish a rapport that will make for an articulate conversation which *informs, educates* and *entertains* the audience. (We shall come across those three words many times in the course of this book.)

Learning to master the techniques demanded by media exposure is not just a vague matter of 'developing company image' or 'improving perceptions in the marketplace' or similar claptrap. It's real. It's measurable in hard cash – to the tune of many millions of pounds.

Consider some case histories which demonstrate the measurable value of making the most of the media. Or, in my first example, of failing to do so ...

## THE POWER OF THE MEDIA

On BBC1, we had launched *Nationwide*, the early-evening programme which was to become the most popular ever screened at that time of day. A film report had featured the township of Millom in Cumberland where the local Co-operative Society store had put up the shutters, and gone into compulsory liquidation. It was a particularly poignant human story, because one of the effects of the collapse was that 24 old people in the town lost all their retirement savings. (There was a strong tradition, especially in the north-west of England, in those days that Co-op members saved their 'divis' – dividends on purchases – to mature in their old age.) The report when transmitted caused quite a stir and, in particular, a protest from a body called the Co-operative Union. They wrote to the governors of the BBC demanding the right of reply.

We were happy to accede to this. We knew our facts were accurate and a good reason for a second bite at the story was journalistically welcome. So the union's president, a certain Lord Jaques, arrived in the studio to be interviewed – 'live', of course – by me.

It was the first item in the programme that night and my opening question could not have been fairer.

'Lord Jaques, what is it you wish to say about our report?'

His reply was a classic example of turning a promotional opportunity into the beginnings of a disaster.

'Well, Michael, I'd like to put the whole story into perspective. There were only 24 old people involved.'

Phrases like 'putting this into perspective' are a dreaded signal that we're in for a game of Dodging The Issue in the worst tradition of political waffle. Worse, much worse, was his assertion about the numbers who had lost their savings.

'But Lord Jaques, surely 24 people are 24 too many. These are human beings who've lost everything they saved.'

'Ah, but let's be clear that this is only one shop in the hundreds of Co-ops around the country.'

Now those of you who watched *Nationwide* will recall that I used to have a bank of television monitors behind me in the studio, linking us to 11 regional studios. And when Lord Jaques made that last assertion, there was an interruption from a Yorkshire viewer in the Leeds studio.

'That's not right,' he said. 'Exactly the same thing happened in our village outside Rotherham last year.'

The interview was going from bad to worse – from the Co-op's point of view.

That evening, as always, I was working with a moulded (supposedly unseen!) earpiece through which the programme director could give me instructions. On this occasion he kept telling me that the interview was being extended and other planned items dropped. Eventually, what had been scheduled as a four-minute item ran to the end of the programme. In that time, poor Lord Jaques and the case for the Co-op lost all shreds of credibility or sympathy.

It was, I suppose, what many would call 'trial by television'. For my own part, I had no qualms about turning the inquisitorial screw because I believed we had a duty (now I'm sounding pompous!) to warn our viewers and expose an organisation that put some people's savings at risk.

However, let's stick to the simple, but stark, facts. Forty-eight hours after that interview was transmitted, it was reported in the press that £20 million had been withdrawn by savers in the Co-operative Bank and the Co-operative Building Society. (Soon afterwards, incidentally, the building society had an emergency general meeting and changed its name ... to the *Nationwide*!)

My purpose in telling the Co-op story in some detail is to underline the point that the impact of something as simple as two people talking in a television studio can be measured in many millions of pounds.

The danger in recounting what happened that evening is that some may come to the conclusion that the media are to be avoided and that businesspeople are on a hiding to nothing if they offer themselves up on the altar of popular exposure.

Nonsense! As we shall see in later chapters, all interview situations offer the opportunity to *profit* from exposure. With skill, the late Lord Jaques could have rescued the reputation of what is, after all, an organisation with a fine social tradition. And we might have seen people next day queuing to place their money with the Co-op!

Let me tell you one more story at this stage which also underlines the multi-million-pound value in using the media adroitly – and at the same time demonstrates how the very worst kind of news 'peg' for an interview can be turned to great advantage.

On a Sunday evening in December 1988 a British Midland Boeing 737 plane crashed on to the M1 near Kegworth in Leicestershire. Forty-seven people were killed.

As the terrible facts filtered through to TV, radio and newspaper newsrooms, the usual frantic efforts to meet deadlines with the story began.

Nothing imaginable could have been more damaging to British Midland. Badly handled by the company's representatives, it could have led to a commercial disaster, too. The anxious questions were painfully obvious. Did this reflect the risks of flying with an independent airline with limited resources? Were the company's maintenance procedures inadequate? Was it true that ...? You can hear the persistent probing of reporters hungry for dramatic headline material.

Very often in cases of crisis like this, company representatives suddenly become 'unavailable for comment' – or hide behind the old excuse that legal actions may ensue, making the issue *sub judice* and so preventing company spokespersons from commenting or answering questions.

In the case of the Kegworth crash, British Midland's attitude was entirely different – and, in my view, wholly admirable. It was also an outstanding example of exploiting the power of communication; of turning a crisis into a public relations opportunity.

Within an hour or so of the crash, I remember sitting at home and watching a special BBC news bulletin which included an interview with British Midland boss (now Sir) Michael Bishop. Truthful, honest, caring, informative, he was the very model of the skilful interviewee. He told us all he knew and more – like the arrangements his team had already made to inform relatives of the known facts and fly them to East Midlands Airport.

It was masterly.

Immediate media response was almost without exception sympathetic and supportive. I cannot recall seeing or hearing any of the harmful theorising by 'experts' that so often follows similar disasters. Indeed, *News at Ten* a couple of days later broadcast a major feature on a 'day in the life of' Mr Bishop and his team which had the effect (for this viewer, at least) of exciting admiration and respect for the airline.

And the measurable value of all this media exposure? It was later reported that the passenger loading of British Midland's scheduled services had *increased* by 10 per cent in the period immediately following the disaster!

There's another way of computing the worth of media time and that's assessing the cost of buying it.

If you want to promote your company or market your products on television, take a deep breath and check the corporate bank balance first: it will need to be particularly healthy. The cost of producing a TV commercial (that's before you have bought transmission time) is obviously immensely variable. Some global corporations may spend a quarter of a million on a 30-second production; a thousand pounds a second is a modest price for computer graphics on tape or film. But it would be reasonable to estimate the cost of a run-of-the-mill commercial, including its showing nationally at peak times, as at least £500,000. Radio and press advertising costs less, of course, but the cost per listener or reader is probably on a par.

So what is the value to your company of, say, a three-minute interview in which you succeed in promoting your message or your product? Almost incalculable!

I like to imagine a TV programme researcher phoning a business executive with an invitation to appear that evening. What that call really says is: I have a cheque here made out to your company. Would you like to come into the studio and cash it?

Of course you would! And yet ... there are many businesspeople who would turn down the opportunity. And many more who, through lack of training or proper preparation, take it and then fail to cash the cheque. This book is all about cashing the cheque.

When I conduct media training sessions with groups of four or five people, I always begin the practical work with a 'simple' exercise. I ask my pupils to prepare for a TV interview as part of a series on careers. I explain that the series is transmitted in the late evening and encourage them to consider the implications of that: viewers will clearly be parents and their sons or daughters who are seriously hungry for information and guidance. At the same time, they need to be helped in a lively, entertaining manner. Otherwise, they'll fall asleep! In my exercise, the career path in question will always be in the profession or business which my pupils practise.

Easy! No unsettling controversies to contend with. No difficult ethical issues. No cause for any aggressive interviewer to expose malpractice. Just cash that cheque!

And yet the proportion of pupils who succeed in that basic aim is small indeed. Time and time again they'll provide an interview in which they forget even to mention the name of their own firm, let alone promote it. They're consumed with all the negative thoughts: must not make a fool of myself, or get my facts wrong, or dry up, or ...

There's another measure of the impact of the media which underlines the value of television or video in particular, and the importance of learning how to make the most of the medium. Research in the United States back in the 1970s – especially at the University of Massachusetts – can be summarised in this way.

People of average intelligence who read, let's say a thousand words of well-written, graphically illustrated printed matter on any subject, will be found when tested to have absorbed roughly 10 per cent of the content. If, however, the same information is purveyed through the ear – perhaps on radio or on a sound tape recording, with music and sound effects to aid the communication technique – the absorption rate will double. That's impressive – but 20 per cent is still not very much!

Now take the information and communicate it through moving pictures plus sound – and the rate jumps to 60 per cent, or six times the impact of the printed word.

That is certainly not to deny the value of the printed or spoken word – but it surely emphasises the need to learn how to profit from all the media if you really want to get your message across.

There's a further bonus, which has nothing to do with money or marketing. It's the thrill of it all! Develop the skills discussed in the following pages and you will set your pulse racing, literally.

Some years ago on *Tomorrow's World*, Raymond Baxter carried out an experiment which I later repeated myself. Simply put, it showed that during a 'live' transmission, a presenter's pulse rate remains steady at only four or five beats above the normal. (It may jump if something goes wrong on air – like a film insert failing to materialise or a sound link breaking down – but that will cause only a temporary blip.) At the end of the programme, signing off 'until the next time' and as the closing music and titles are run, the pulse rate soars – in my case, to something like 122 beats per minute.

There are various explanations for this. My own, naive, theory is that adrenalin keeps the pulse subdued when we're performing – and then 'lets go' when the show's over.

Whatever the explanation, the experience is extraordinarily stimulating – but very far removed from nervous tension. That is something we're going to learn to conquer, too ...

## CHAPTER TWO

# Accentuate the positive ... with a little help from your friend!

The cosmetics of media presentation and interview techniques are simple enough. Appropriate dress, good posture, a steady eyeline, the warmth of a smile ... We'll examine all these and more later. But they will be of little avail if the basic attitude to this kind of exposure is wrong.

Think of the interview as a 'grilling' or the studio chair rather like the one in the dentist's and you'll throw away a great opportunity. Regard your interviewer as 'the enemy' and you'll be shot to pieces.

On the other hand, if you approach an interview as a heaven-sent chance to promote yourself and your cause – worth a fortune, as we've seen – your attitude will underpin your performance. You'll look as though you're proud of what you practise or make or sell.

There's a widely held view that media people only have an interest in the 'bad news', that they like to see their 'victims' discomfited. Partly that stems from a common failure to accept a question for what it is – not an aggressive harrying of an interviewee, but the most effective way of eliciting facts.

If the price of gas goes up, I may want to ask an industry representative why. Is it necessary? Why couldn't it be avoided? How is it justified when so much is spent on advertising or on executives' salaries?

These are not loaded questions. They don't reflect my opinion (which I would never reveal, anyway). And they're certainly not unfair – merely a reflection of the questions which I believe are in the minds of my viewers, listeners or readers.

There may be perfectly reasonable, factual answers to all the questions. If the interviewee provides those answers – and does so in an informative, entertaining and even educative manner – then we have a valuable contribution to what may be a national debate (and incidentally the industry or company concerned will have improved its image in the eyes of customers).

If, on the other hand, the answers are woolly and unconvincing, delivered in a boring and ineffective way, the interview will have failed in its purpose – and *I'll* be on the carpet! I'll be the one blamed by my editor for failing to get to the bottom of an important issue.

This point will arise again and again as we examine relationships with the media: the professional wants you to 'perform' well – for his own sake.

Let me tell you a story, as it were in parenthesis, which illustrates this from an interviewer's point of view. It relates to the time in the early 1960s when a major increase was proposed in MPs' salaries – an emotive subject and one which was tailor-made for a lively debate (more vulgarly, a punch-up!) in the *Panorama* studio. The 'contestants' were Labour's Tom Driberg and the Tory Charles Curran. It was 1963 and, as it turned out, the last months of the Conservative government. I asked Curran how he could justify paying MPs so much more when the country was facing financial difficulties. He provided the lucid, literate answer I'd have expected from a long-standing Member who was also a reputed journalist. Turning to Driberg, I simply asked his reaction, complacently sure that it would be an apoplectic tirade against Curran's position. But he agreed with it! In my earpiece, the director intoned: 'Six minutes to go.'

It was probably the worst discussion I ever conducted on television. I had no pithy questions to stimulate the pair and they were disinclined to enliven an argument. After we came off the air and retired to the green room for the usual glass of wine and cold chicken leg, Grace Wyndham Goldie – the awesome and legendary

# ACCENTUATE THE POSITIVE

lady who 'invented' BBC TV current affairs output – took me to one side.

'Michael, what will you do when your present contract expires? Take up farming, perhaps?' She was withering.

It looked like the end of my career in television. It taught me a lesson I've never forgotten – that it's my job to help interviewees to perform at their best. I must fashion questions which encourage expansive answers. (Very basic technique calls for questions which begin with words like 'how' or 'why'.) I must do my homework, so that in the event of an interview running out of steam – as it did that evening with Curran and Driberg – I should be prepared to pursue other lines of questioning.

If the interviewee performs in a dull and seemingly disinterested way, I may inject an emotive question deliberately to rile – and so to bring some life into our encounter, for both our sakes!

There are times, which I've experienced often enough, when the interviewee dries up altogether, literally struck dumb with nerves. In such cases the professional will always come to the rescue by 'taking the blame'. Thus: 'I'm sorry, perhaps I didn't make my question clear. Let me put it another way ...'

But let's not go over the top about the supportive role of the interviewer. I grant you that there are times when he may become decidedly antipathetic – if you're clearly telling lies, for instance, or deliberately dodging the question, or (in extreme circumstances) covering up criminal activities.

If you *are* a dubious character with something to hide, this book will bring you no comfort! The chances of deluding a vigilant press or professional broadcasting techniques nowadays are happily slim. Especially in television and radio, it's not simply what you say that reveals the truth. That look in the eyes or tremor in the voice can mean more than words.

I remember one of the most frightening spells of my TV reporting life when I set out to expose the nefarious activities of the Kray twins in London's East End – before they were finally apprehended by the police.

As often happens in these kinds of investigation, I made contact with Ronald Kray in the simplest way – by phoning him! I explained that we were looking into allegations of a protection racket in the pubs in his patch. He told me that this was absolute nonsense and that he was prepared to meet me to give me the facts.

It was agreed that I should take the tube, alone, to Whitechapel where I would be met. The story from here begins to read like second-rate melodrama, but I promise you it's all true.

'How will I recognise your man?'

'Don't worry about that. He'll recognise you.'

'But how?'

'You'll see.'

In the event, I left the station to find myself confronted by an extremely large black man with shaven head and dauntingly muscular frame. There was no doubting his role as he silently gestured to me to follow him into a pub along the road. We went in – and there, sitting alone in a sea of empty chairs in the café-style saloon bar, sat Ronald Kray.

He motioned me to sit opposite him at a small table while the bodyguard friend took up position at the back of the bar.

Ronald was a real smoothie. He seemed sincerely concerned to set the record straight about the East End community. *His* community. He talked to me about all the charity work he and his twin brother Reggie did in the area. He showed me photographs of the two of them presenting trophies at charity boxing matches, and press stories about their various charitable activities.

And then he made a startling suggestion. 'Bring your camera crew here on Friday night,' he said, 'and talk to anybody you like in the local pubs. Ask them about the so-called protection racket. You won't be molested.'

It was significant, of course, that he was demonstrating his influence in the area by making promises of 'safe passage' for me and my crew wherever we went.

Anyway, I took him up on his offer and the following Friday began a tour of local pubs with cameraman and sound recordist. At the first, I asked the landlord:

'What threats have been made to you by thugs seeking contributions for protection?'

## ACCENTUATE THE POSITIVE

'None at all. There has never been any threat to me or the pub. I don't know what you're talking about.'

Round to the next pub. Same question. Same answer:

'None at all. There has never been any threat to me or the pub ...'

In pub after pub, the willingness of the landlord to be interviewed was remarkable. And the answer to my question was exactly the same.

I made my excuses, as they say, and left the Krays' domain. I had failed to secure any evidence of criminal practices.

A principle for the baddies? An example of how to defeat the media investigator at his own game? I think not. The precise repetition of the Kray line in every establishment told its own story as clearly as any 'confession'. The word-for-word denials when edited together become affirmations! I make no claim to having brought the Krays to justice – their murderous activities required years of painstaking and dangerous police work – but investigative journalism did play its part.

By retelling that story, I'm trying to stress some lessons about media interviewing:

1. Vanity will get you nowhere. People like the criminal Krays (or, dare I say it, respectable political figures) who think they can cynically manipulate the channels of communication through their personal magnetism will always fail to do so.

2. The inoffensive reporter is not your friend if you have criminal or anti-social intent. In these circumstances, he'll go for the jugular. Re-read the beginning of this chapter with this in mind!

3. Print, sound and visual techniques don't require bald confessions to destroy a reputation. Often what is not said may do the damage. So can subtler images like shifty eyes or hesitant speech.

One more negative example of media power before we pursue our real intent – how to make the most of the media.

It was in the early 1960s when a young Labour backbencher, Richard (now Lord) Marsh, asked a question in the Commons about the arms trade. He was concerned about dealings in weapons which were bringing what he regarded as immoral earnings to a number of businessmen in this country at a time when savage wars were being fought in countries like the Congo and the Yemen.

I was charged with investigating the story for *Panorama* and in the course of my researches came across an ex-army major who was now an arms trader in Kent. I could hardly believe the conversation I was having with him on the phone ...

'Yes,' he said in answer to my inquiry, 'I sell arms abroad. And I'm proud of it. Don't you go calling me a "merchant of death" or any of that journalist hogwash.'

'Very well, Major. But can you tell me where you sell these weapons?'

'Yes, we're doing very good business in the Congo at the moment. And the Yemen's doing well, too.'

'But which side do you trade with?' I asked, with astonishment that he should be so frank.

'Either side, of course. Anybody who has the money to buy. I'm not concerned with the ethics of it all, if that's what you're getting at. It's good business and that's what matters.'

Hardly daring to ask, I wanted to know if he would be prepared to tell me all this in the studio on Monday evening.

'Of course. I'm not ashamed of it.'

He even agreed to let us visit his arsenal where we filmed guns and ammunition destined for the various war zones.

On air, I confronted him along with Richard Marsh. The altercation went something like this:

'Major, I believe you sell weapons abroad. Can you tell me which countries buy them?'

'Oh, all over the world. Belgium and France are particularly good customers at the moment.'

'What about the Third World? The Congo, perhaps, or the Yemen?'

His answer left me gasping.

'Oh, no, I wouldn't dream of sending arms there.'

On air, in a 'live' programme, the dangers of libel are ever present. I couldn't call him a liar. So what was I to do?

'Major, I have to say that before we came on air you told me that you *did* supply weapons to the factions on both sides in those African countries.'

'No, you must have misunderstood ...'

Look at a transcript of what was said and you might assume that our arms trader 'got away with it'. Not so. The television critics all praised our exposure of this man who, they had no doubt, was denying the truth. They could see his eyes!

Again, I underline the fact that media probing will usually reveal the truth even if it's achieved by means as indeterminate as body language.

You, gentle reader, have no desire to fear this kind of 'trial' because you have nothing to hide. Indeed, your purpose is to promote ... so let's find out how to achieve just that.

CHAPTER THREE
..................

# The most important skill of all ... the art of listening

Of all the skills of personal communication, there's none in my view to be compared with the skill of *listening*.

That is not only true of the interview – it actually applies to *speaking*, too, which may sound like a contradiction in terms but will be explained later!

Let's first look at the essential need to listen intently by taking a typical scenario before a radio or television studio interview.

First, the phone call comes from a programme researcher. 'Hello, I'm Sally Smith from *TV Newswide*. I wonder if you can help. We're running an item tonight about warranty schemes for household goods – washing machines, cookers, that sort of thing. I understand you're marketing director of a company which provides these sort of warranties. Can you tell me how they work, so that we can get our facts straight?'

It's a straightforward request, with no hidden traps – although your warranty scheme has received some bad publicity recently. However, it's likely that Ms Smith will also have in mind the possibility of asking you to appear on the programme, so you need to be immediately alert to the opportunity for 'cashing the cheque' that all interviews present. In answering her research questions, you must work extremely hard to sell yourself.

She, you may be sure, will be listening intently. Are your answers to her simple but probing questions lucid, succinct,

## MAKING THE MOST OF THE MEDIA

informative? Do you have an attractive manner of delivery, an authoritative voice? If you pass these kinds of test, the invitation will probably follow. 'Would you be prepared to come into the studio tonight to be interviewed?'

Would you, indeed! She's offering you the chance of a free commercial for the company and, incidentally, for your own career prospects ... provided you handle it skilfully. But first you need to establish the format of the proposed item. Who will be the interviewer? How will the piece be structured in the studio? Will I be confronting any consumers or complainants?

Above all, you need to be sure that the area of questioning (not the precise questions) will cover issues that come within your own knowledge. There's nothing worse than being faced in a 'live' interview with a question to which you simply don't know the answer because it's not in your field of expertise.

Anyway, if you're satisfied on all these points, you agree to turn up at the studios at the appointed time, probably half an hour or so before transmission – and then you devote all your energies to preparing yourself for the big challenge.

You call in your colleagues and your advisers (like in-house or external public relations consultants) and work out the strategy for exploiting the evening's opportunity.

First, you work out together the questions which are most likely to be asked. This calls for hard work but is not particularly difficult. Your knowledge of the issue is greater than that of the programme team and so you may be fairly sure that you can list even more possible questions – including the controversial ones – than they can!

Armed with this list, your next step is to determine the most effective answers ... and then to develop them to your own advantage. Always they should be truthful. And the 'commercials' should be justifiable, in the context of the discussion, rather than blatant self-promotion which will antagonise both interviewer and viewers.

After several hours' work, you should be ready for anything as far as the content of the coming interview is concerned. (We'll be analysing other skills and how you handle relationships with the TV team later.)

## THE MOST IMPORTANT SKILL OF ALL ... THE ART OF LISTENING

On air, the first question is put to you: 'Mr Bloggs, your own company has suffered some damaging publicity recently ...'

Yes, you're ready for this one! You put on your warmest smile, settle back confidently in your chair and catch a glimpse of yourself in a studio monitor as you wait for the interviewer to finish the question you'd been expecting and launch into your well-rehearsed answer.

'Ah, thank you for the opportunity to put the record straight. My company, Household Wares Ltd. (managed to get the name in already!) was found to have acted quite properly – indeed, generously – by an independent institute which examined the case of the dripping taps to which you no doubt refer. And I can tell you ...' (you warm to your subject and start to turn the interview into a promotional exercise).

And you have failed disastrously. Because you haven't *listened*.

In fact, while you were admiring yourself in the monitor and waiting to deliver your rehearsed response, the question you didn't hear went something like this: 'Mr Bloggs, your own company has suffered some damaging publicity recently. We'll come to that later. But first – can you explain what the industry actually means by a warranty?'

By failing to listen to what you were actually being asked, you've ruined any chance of securing the viewers' acceptance of your credibility – and therefore any impact from your promotional message.

'Why doesn't he answer the question?' we can hear from millions of your potential customers at home. And, of course, the interviewer will emphasise your self-inflicted discomfort by having to say something like: 'Yes but, with respect, would you please answer my question?'

It's not even enough to take in the precise wording of a question: you must be sensitive to the intonations and implications, too. (No printed transcription of an ad lib discussion will ever convey the impressions of the actual event – another example of the added impact of sound and moving pictures.)

The intensity of effort needed to listen intently throughout an interview, and then to respond instantly and effectively, calls for a degree of quick-thinking concentration beyond anything else you will experience. It is no exaggeration to say that completing a four-minute 'live' interview to the best of your ability will leave you more drained than a normal full day's work.

But the effort is well worth it!

Consider, too, the art of listening even in the circumstances of making a speech – to a press conference, perhaps, or at that business club lunch or industry society dinner.

Up on your feet, very much on your own, you have a captive audience and no one to ask you awkward questions (though at a press conference, they'll come later). So what are you supposed to be listening to? Your mute audience!

In other words, you must develop the skill of 'listening' to what may be called the 'vibes' coming from those in front of you. Are their faces glazed with boredom? Are they beginning to whisper to each other? Are their glasses tinkling with increasing frequency as they attend more to their drinks than to what you're saying? Are all these messages telling you that you've pitched your speech at the wrong level – that you're too serious or too lighthearted for the occasion? (The serious business group probably doesn't want a heavy diatribe at its dinner on December 22 when husbands and wives are invited. By the same token, industrialists who have paid a significant fee to attend a conference on, say, management communication techniques, will not be over-enamoured by a flip speech full of 'funny' stories.)

As for 'listening' to the audience's messages indicating that you may be outstaying your welcome, let me underline, in passing, the great virtues of brevity. During my media training sessions, I usually ask which of the assembled pupils has ever attended a function at which the speech has been too *short*. I have yet to hear of one!

But what's to be done if you are taking in those vibes and you realise you're on the wrong track? You have in front of you typed pages of a speech which you've prepared with great care. How are you to change it all as you stand there?

The pat answer is that you throw away your notes and deliver the rest of your speech off the cuff.

I know many very clever, hugely successful, articulate business leaders who'd rather die! However, I still recommend those who

## THE MOST IMPORTANT SKILL OF ALL ... THE ART OF LISTENING

are going to be addressing audiences regularly to try to develop the art of speaking ad lib. It's hard work. It means mentally rehearsing a logically progressive theme (not learning the actual words) over and over again until you have it clear-cut in the mind.

The best way to do this, in my experience, is to write down five or six one-word 'headlines' of the argument you want to pursue. See whether they make a sensible progression, building to a rational conclusion. Then commit them to memory. You may also like to write them down on a small card which can be easily referred to if memory fails when you're standing there and the mind goes completely blank.

Developing this skill will have two main effects. It will help you to get across your message much more effectively by using conversational rather than written English (see next chapter). And it will gradually develop your confidence in changing tack when that vital 'listening' process tells you it's necessary to do so.

Practise these skills over the years and you may come to be irritated by those who say: 'It's easy for you. Speaking in public comes naturally.'

Don't let that rankle. They're paying you the highest possible compliment!

CHAPTER FOUR

• • • • • • • • • • • • • • • •

# Born bilingual ... and the need for simple English

When I joined *Panorama,* back in the 1960s, my first assignments were in the United States. With me were Christopher Ralling, destined to become one of the most respected of the BBC's documentary directors (*The Voyage of the Beagle* was one of the most memorable) and Eric Durschmeid, the brilliant and brave cameraman who was to make an international reputation for his work especially in battle areas like the Congo and Vietnam.

It was a memorable trip. It began with a terrible story in Birmingham, Alabama where little black children were killed by a bomb planted in a negro church Sunday school hall. (For me, the worst aspect of that was working with a white sound recordist who kept referring to the victims as 'nigras' and who claimed to have lost the sound tape so that we were prevented from recording the most moving words of the preacher at the funeral service.)

We also travelled to Houston, Texas, to cover the awesome developments towards the conquest of space. And, in Canada, we reported on the violence behind the Quebec Separatist movement (at that time similar to the later excesses of the IRA in Northern Ireland). It was during filming in Montreal that we three were arrested, put behind bars in the city gaol, and next morning found guilty on a trumped-up charge of 'trespassing on Federal Government property'. It was my first experience of the fact that star billing as a radio or television reporter is neither as cosy nor as glamorous as the publicity spotlight may suggest.

Back home after a month-long tour, I found myself the subject of some most flattering exposure in the papers. Maurice Wiggin in the *Sunday Times*, I remember, referred to me as a 'terrier' in the true tradition of *Panorama*. My head was in danger of becoming visibly swollen when I was called to the office of the programme's editor, David Wheeler.

He is a quiet man but firm. For some unaccountable reason, I remember his habit in those days of tapping a silver pencil on the notepad he carried everywhere before delivering a broadside. Quite simply he said: 'You are banned from using adjectives in any commentary you write from now on.'

I was stunned. It seemed an impossible, indeed brutal (there I go with the adjectives!) instruction. In fact, it was the most valuable single piece of training I have ever received as a journalist. It stemmed from my popular newspaper background – a tradition of wrapping everything in journalese. Everything was 'dramatic' or 'sensational' or 'tragic'. The never-ending use of the adjectives, of course, devalues them and ultimately renders them meaningless.

Why do I recount this story? Because I want to suggest a rule that's equally stark: when talking to the media – or, indeed in business meetings – try not to use any words of more than two syllables. It will not be easy. After all, the very words *simplicity* and *communication* break the rule. But try. Your ability to 'get through' to other people will be greatly enhanced. You will be pursuing objectives which we're going to examine in this chapter.

First of all, the basics. When you're approached by a media reporter, your response will be spoken, not written. And there's a world of difference.

All of us are in a sense bilingual. Some of us are very clever and speak several languages but all of us use two – written and spoken English. I have a view that they should not be all that different, but the fact is that you are likely to use different words in an office memo from the ones you will use face to face with a colleague. Thus the memo will use words like 'commence' or 'prior to' instead of the conversational 'begin' or 'before'. The written words, when spoken, are actually a barrier to communication: you would never use them socially and they jar when you're talking through the medium of a journalistic interview.

Strangely, we are all prone to a kind of chemistry in the artificial environment of a television or radio studio, or facing the formalities of a newspaper interview. I've never quite understood why, but all the physical paraphernalia involved – the cameras, microphones and other equipment – have the effect of making us speak in 'written' English.

And it's not just the actual words which are affected in this way. The manner in which we use them alters, too.

Bernard Levin provided a notable example of this in one of his essays for *The Times* some years ago when he complained of the way so many people in radio and television pronounced the definite article.

In ordinary conversation we all naturally pronounce 'the' as 'thee' before a vowel and 'th' before words beginning with a consonant. Put us in the surroundings of a studio and so many people – including, sadly, professional commentators – use 'thee' on almost all occasions.

Does that matter? Yes, I think it does. It's a signal to the listener or viewer that what we're saying is part of a 'performance' – an artificial, affected way of speaking which by its nature weakens the speaker's credibility. It is not 'natural'.

There's another, increasingly common, threat to communication effectiveness. Jargon. It has always been with us in the business world, though somehow the burgeoning of computer-speak has made it worse. We no longer meet people. We 'interface' with them.

I'm not being superior about this: jargon is rife in the media business, too! My own company, for example, produces videos for industry and commerce – for marketing, training, internal communications and so forth. Most people would call them 'corporate' videos. But what does the word 'corporate' actually mean? According to my Oxford dictionary, it means variously 'united into one body ... corpulent ... forming a body politic or corporation'. So why not, simply, company videos?

Different trades and professions have their own forms of jargon. They're used as a kind of shorthand, in the unquestioning belief that they are easily understood by everybody in their specialist world. If I advise people not to use their jargon through the popular media, on the basis that lay people won't understand it, I'm not likely to be contradicted. But I have a much more difficult job in persuading them that *they don't understand each other*!

And they'll never know. After all, if you use a jargon phrase to a colleague, there is normally no way of telling that the meaning you are transmitting is the meaning that is being received by your listener. Human vanity comes into this equation, too. Thus, if a youngster in my own profession uses a piece of jargon while talking to me, my pride may find it difficult to admit that I don't understand what it means!

Let me give you a practical example to bolster my contention about 'insider' jargon ...

I was producing a group video for ICI in the days when industrial relations were tense, even though this great corporation had a fine record of industrial democracy – at least by the standards of the 1970s.

We had arranged to record a session in which employees at various levels in the group would put questions to the chairman (then Sir Maurice Hodgson). To show that there would be no management manipulation of this internal communication exercise, it was bravely agreed that the session would be recorded with a guarantee that there would be no editing afterwards and that the chairman would not be shown the questions in advance.

One of the consequences of this arrangement was that the employees needed, in my judgement, to be helped in framing their questions – not only for their own sakes but also so that Sir Maurice could fairly be expected to understand what they were getting at!

So we arranged a lunch-hour meeting which I chaired with the ICI head of personnel in attendance. At one point I turned to a well-known militant operative from the Billingham plant on Teesside. Let's call him Bill.

'What do you propose to ask the chairman, Bill?'

'Well, what I want to know is – are we going upstream or are we going downstream in our operations next year?'

## BORN BILINGUAL ... AND THE NEED FOR SIMPLE ENGLISH

Oh, dear, jargon raising its ugly head – and from someone who didn't take kindly to criticism from clever Dicks like me. I trod lightly.

'Fine, Bill – a good question. But can I suggest that not everybody in the audience [incidentally, 190 000 employees around the world] will understand that word upstream.'

'Well I understand it, and my mates understand it, so that's good enough for me.'

Ouch! I was wondering how to cope with this when the head of personnel interjected by explaining to me exactly what 'upstream' meant in ICI terms.

'Oh no it doesn't,' thundered Bill – and went on to give a totally different definition of the word.

Enough said?

It did strike me at the time that in countless meetings in consultative committees over the years in ICI (and, of course, the same applied to every other company in the land) crucial negotiations were being conducted between two sides using jargon words which had quite different meanings to each of them. So much for delicate nuances of argument!

But back to basics and the great merits of simple language. It may be tempting at times to show off, to try to impress your audience with fancy words – usually long ones. That is not clever. There's only one thing that matters: are you being understood?

That should be the rule for the professional interviewer, too. If it's not observed – if you don't understand the question being put to you – say so! It's not your job to protect the presenter; you have a hard enough job protecting yourself. (We'll be taking a closer look at bad presenters later.)

Practise the use of simple words in all your activities – not just when you're talking through the media but in the office and even at home, too. It's not unusual for me to receive phone calls from people I've trained in the past that go something like this:

'Hello. You won't remember me, but I want to tell you that all you said about simple speech has helped me enormously.'

'Oh, I didn't know you'd been on the box.'

'No, I don't mean that. It's helped me at work. Colleagues and customers have been saying that I'm getting through to them much better than I used to.'

> Try that challenge: no words of more than two syllables. Simplicity. If you see what I mean!

# CHAPTER FIVE

## The right royal way to influence but not manipulate ... and how to develop a relationship

I suppose the British royal family provide some of the best examples of how to – and how *not* to – influence the media advantageously.

The younger members of the clan have made countless mistakes, often stemming from an arrogant assumption that they can *manipulate* the media (a rather different concept!). I believe that all their troubles, in public-image terms, began when they first opened their doors to the reporters and cameramen and sound recordists. With an antiquated belief in their own divine right and imperviousness to the kind of criticism the rest of us may face, they thought the media would dance to their tune. They were disastrously, possibly even fatally, wrong.

If only they had followed the example of Queen Elizabeth the Queen Mother! She knew, and never let herself deviate from, the way to earn respect and even love. A personal story will illustrate my case ...

In 1985 I embarked on the job of writing and directing an hour-long programme to be called, simply, *Queen Mother*. Obviously I needed her support and that of her personal staff if I was to secure interviews with key people and permission to film in private locations. (The loyalty she generated from employees and friends meant that nobody would talk unless they first established that she was happy for them to do so.)

I therefore began my researches by visiting Clarence House. It was like stepping back some distance in time. The copper at the front door was almost a caricature: 'Good morning, sir, and what brings you here? Come to see Her Majesty, have you?'

He let me into the front hall where Major John Griffin greeted me and took me to meet Sir Martin Gilliat in his almost Dickensian office with high-backed leather chairs.

'It seems a little early for a proper drink,' said the major, almost regretfully, I thought (the time was 11.30). 'May we offer you some light refreshment? A cup of tea? Bovril, perhaps?'

Bovril, I said, was a delightful idea.

'Ah, well, why don't we get on with our meeting and have a proper drink afterwards?'

It was one of the swiftest, but most fruitful, meetings I have ever attended. It was certainly purposeful – with the major and Sir Martin clearly eager to open doors for me and smooth my path by putting me in touch with people I most wanted to meet: people like Lady Strathmore and Viscount Thurso in her beloved Scotland; thriller writer Dick Francis (who rode her horse Devon Loch when it collapsed within 24 yards of the 1956 Grand National finishing post); fisherfolk; soldiers; gardeners ...

It was arranged that I could attend, and film, the annual flower show in Windsor Park's village hall which she had attended every year since she lived in the village as Duchess of York.

The rules were strict enough: She would not give an interview. Indeed, she had *never* given an interview throughout her life despite almost daily requests from newspapers and broadcasting stations all over the world. However, we would be allowed to follow her around the hall as she examined the vegetables and the blooms on show. (When the filming took place, my cameraman became rather carried away and got so close to Her Majesty that I feared we would be taken away to the Tower for importuning. At one point, she turned away from a villager who had been showing her his prizewinning potatoes and nearly collided with the camera. Untroubled, she paused and gave the most captivating smile, right into the lens, and proceeded to the next stall.)

## THE RIGHT ROYAL WAY TO INFLUENCE BUT NOT MANIPULATE

Now you may feel that I was naively overcome by all this – that my journalistic judgement was unbalanced by all the old-world courtesies and graciousness of the Queen Mother's retinue. But I think not. In producing what turned out to be a documentary loud in singing her praises, we were simply reflecting the honest evidence about someone we concluded was 'surely the best-loved woman in the world'.

It would not have been clever – and certainly not faithful to the patent facts – to have produced a cynical, abusive portrait. The supportive response to my requests by Major Griffin and Sir Martin brought reward for all of us – and in that story is a clue to how the media may be influenced rather than manipulated.

Let's put all that in more mundane terms. Let's look at how to respond to media inquiries in day-to-day matters.

When you are approached to help with a topical story, respond with eagerness! Offer the researcher or reporter additional information (or even a cup of Bovril!). Suggest ways of making the 'story' more interesting and entertaining – perhaps with illustrations or graphics that may be at your disposal. Taking that attitude, you will right from the start 'make friends' and begin the vital process of turning media exposure into powerful opportunity.

The opposite reaction can be most damaging. Refuse to talk to the press, or turn down requests to state your case in a studio, and you are planting dangerous seeds in sensitive minds. What are they hiding? Why are they scared to face the cameras?

Take a leaf out of the Clarence House book and you won't go far wrong!

But don't try to be too clever. Courtesy and responsiveness are important weapons in your armoury when seeking to purvey an admirable image, but aggressive PR promotion techniques – 'selling' your image hard – can easily backfire.

In my days on *Nationwide*, I suffered what became known as the 'PR hour'. It lasted each day between approximately 4 p.m. and 5 p.m. and it took the form of phone calls from obviously well-lunched PR 'executives' (the bullshit extended even to their own job descriptions!) who would ring up to suggest some fatuous programme idea.

MAKING THE MOST OF THE MEDIA

'My client is putting a Page Three girl on a horse, to ride down Park Lane in the nude tomorrow. Would you like to cover this for your programme? She'll be wearing a wig to hide the naughty bits, of course, but it should make an exciting sequence for you.'

'But what's the peg?' I'd ask, dreading the answer.

'We're opening a new salon for Godiva Hair Stylists.'

I would put the phone down in anger – angry that this so-called professional should demean the programme by assuming we might even consider such a crazy idea; angry because we had only an hour or two before transmission and were therefore frantically busy writing scripts and researching issues in preparation for interviews; and angry because some company was actually paying good money to employ people like the caller, in the honest but naive belief that they were experts in selling us promotional stories.

The skilful PR person would know better than to call up a famously 'live' programme at the very time that presenters and producers were fighting the clock to get the show ready on time.

None of this is to say that PR people (the truly professional ones, that is) are resented by the media or can't help their companies to seek good promotional opportunities. I can think of many occasions where a genuinely bright idea has earned its proper reward.

Perhaps the most effective project in my time was the annual *Nationwide* Nurse of the Year competition, suggested by a public relations consultant to Reckitt and Colman, manufacturers of Dettol disinfectant. It had so much going for it: nurses, after all, are guaranteed to attract viewers' admiration. There was, too, the developing excitement of a national competition; the human stories of devotion to those in need; and the regional rivalry that sprang from the early 'rounds' being conducted in our provincial studios.

Something like 11 million people switched on to *Nationwide* every evening in those days. At the grand final, which occupied the whole duration of the programme, there was a panel of judges chaired by ... the managing director of Reckitt and Colman Pharmaceuticals.

## THE RIGHT ROYAL WAY TO INFLUENCE BUT NOT MANIPULATE

And the prize? A magnificent sword. The Dettol sword, of course!

Another popular competition we ran was to find the *Nationwide* Cook of the Realm. This time the top judge was the editor of *Woman's Realm*.

The BBC, of course, has strict rules prohibiting advertising on its airwaves – yet these examples of clever marketing were judged wholly acceptable.

So the lesson of this chapter is, quite simply, that you can effectively promote your business or yourself – provided you take the trouble to *help* your target media, ideally in the most professional manner.

CHAPTER SIX

# Better the devil you know ... behind the scenes

One of the most helpful ways of learning how to influence media people is to go behind the scenes and find out not only how, but why, they behave as they do.

Programmes and papers vary, of course, in their precise methods. Some have different target audiences – from the television current affairs magazine to the consumer watchdog on radio to a mountain of newspapers and magazines devoted to every interest under the sun. But they are nearly all driven by very similar 'journalistic' rules. So the scenario I'm about to relate, although set in a television framework, will provide a guide to most media practices.

Each weekday morning, early, the *TV Newswide* team – editor, producers, reporters, researchers – meet to discuss the content of their programme which will be transmitted in the evening. They will have all watched the breakfast TV output, then listened to radio bulletins and current affairs magazines on their way to work. They're knee-deep in newspapers and magazines which have been combed for stories: most of the topics they will cover tonight will be 'follow-ups' to things already published although there will also be 'diary items' – that's to say, fixed events like political debates, major business AGMs, celebrities due to visit the country, book launches and so on. In each case, the team will discuss new 'angles'

# MAKING THE MOST OF THE MEDIA

to attract viewers. The editor will be looking for a 'mix' of stories to ensure that the programme is well balanced.

Occasionally, unexpected fresh ideas will emerge from the meeting. One morning in the *Nationwide* office, for instance, we were joined as usual by all the news editors in 11 regional studios on a sound 'hook-up'. What were they proposing to feature that evening?

'Well, up here in Leeds ...' began our man there.

'You mean *down* there,' interjected Newcastle.

'You're not pretending you're northerners are you?' joked Glasgow.

'That's rich coming from southerners in Glasgow,' scoffed Aberdeen.

In no time at all, a little jocularity developed into a passionate and clearly deeply felt argument about who could properly claim to be a northerner. In our London production office we sat back and listened in some astonishment to these adult professionals working themselves into a frenzy – until the editor broke into the debate to say we'd do an item that night on the subject. On air, I stood in front of a map of the United Kingdom, asking the question 'Where does the North begin?' moving a magnetic line up and down as a live argument raged between our regional studios. And next day the phone calls and letters from viewers made us acutely aware that they really cared about the answer.

But I digress. Back to our *TV Newswide* meeting. One of the stories in the morning papers suggests that a pain-killing drug which has been on the market and prescribed by doctors for some time may have harmful side-effects. It's an obvious topic for that night, a matter of serious public concern. How should it be tackled? It's likely to run throughout the day on news bulletins, rival TV programmes, evening papers. Is there a new angle? That may emerge as the day progresses and researchers get to work. The editor deploys his troops: 'Mary, you find out the history of this drug – when it was licensed here, what has been its history overseas, what questions have been asked about its safety before?

Bill, you handle the item and interviews in the studio. John, produce some graphics when we've got the facts. Sue, line up someone from the manufacturers – maybe the marketing manager but go to the top if it looks like developing into a major scandal. Check with Mary on what the Department of Health are saying and line up the minister and opposition shadow if there are party political implications.'

You'll note that in all this there's no injunction to build the news into a scare story. Nor to find a gibbering idiot from the pharmaceutical company who'll make a fool of himself in front of the cameras. Despite what some cynics appear to believe, that is not the intention of the programme-makers. They want an interviewee who will perform as well as possible, so that the item will – remember? – inform, educate and entertain the audience (The word 'entertain' incidentally, does not suggest singing and dancing! It's to be achieved by a lively delivery, animation, good body language and similar techniques we'll be learning later.)

Anyway, as the story develops during the day, new facts will come to life calling perhaps for a different approach. The interviewee asked early in the day to appear may be 'stood down' at the last minute: I always found it particularly embarrassing to tell people – some of whom might have actually arrived at the studio – that they were no longer needed. That's the way of the 'running story'.

If you're the lucky one, you arrive at the *TV Newswide* studio in good time – possibly half an hour before transmission – for any necessary make-up or briefing from researcher or presenter. And the first thing that strikes you is how helpful everybody is. They really seem to want you to be at ease so that you can give of your best.

You'll be offered a drink. (Accept only non-alcoholic!) You'll be taken to the make-up room – though these days you're unlikely to need more than a dusting of powder over a shiny forehead, or a comb through unruly hair.

In the studio itself you'll be in the care of the floor manager who will provide you with a glass of water (not for drinking in my book!) and ask if you're comfortable and have everything you need.

Yes, he really wants to know. It's a part of his job to see that you have the best possible aids to performing well. It should also be stressed that he will welcome any requests or anxieties you may express. For instance, if you're seated in a swivel chair which makes you ill at ease because it's not very stable, say so. He may not replace it (especially if it is 'designer furniture' which is an integral part of the whole studio set) but he will certainly respond to your anxieties, perhaps by locking-off the swivel mechanism. If you feel uncomfortably low, ask for a cushion. You won't be considered a silly amateur fusspot. On the contrary, the production team will welcome the evidence that you're approaching the interview with professional concern.

For the programme team themselves, the drug story has developed – and may even change on air. As the seconds remorselessly tick by until transmission time, an army of individuals attend to their own specialised duties.

The editor checks through the script to make sure that the coverage is balanced and informative but also fresh and appealing to viewers.

Some researchers are still trying to unearth new facts about the drug which may be injected into the script at the last minute – or even on air. Others are monitoring the Press Association tapes, news broadcasts and competing current affairs programmes to make sure they're not missing a trick.

The studio director, production assistant, vision mixer, technical engineers, camera operators and all the rest of a considerable team are checking their own responsibilities and rehearsing the planned shots. They range from the novices to people of long experience, but they all have the same feeling of excitement (however carefully they may try to hide it) as the transmission is about to begin. 'Tension mounts' is a joke phrase. But it really does!

The presenter has done his homework – within limits. (He may have other subjects to tackle in the same programme and the library cuttings about this drug may be sparse or inaccurate.) He has prepared his questions – just as you have worked on your answers! – but he knows that the only question which really matters is the first one. After that, the course of the interview – if it is to be an intelligent one – may develop in many unexpected directions.

You will observe his preparations and may learn a thing or two for your own benefit as you do so. For instance, in my own early days in the business I was privileged to watch the great Richard Dimbleby at work. And I suppose the overwhelming impression was of a man who knew through decades of experience that it was the little things that mattered most. This man who was probably the most respected TV and radio commentator in the world – friend of kings and queens, presidents and prime ministers – could be seen each Monday evening before *Panorama* went out, busying himself with bits of paper and Sellotape and ballpoint pens. He would scribble a name or a number on a piece of paper and stick it under the lens of a camera he'd be working to. I've seen him write the name of a renowned personage on the palm of his hand or the cuff of his shirt – because he knew that it is always possible to forget the simplest of facts in the pressurised circumstances of a 'live' broadcast.

'Stand by, studio.' The countdown begins. Ten, nine, eight ...

The professionals are ready.

Are you?

# CHAPTER SEVEN

# Television ... the art of persuasion ... and projection

Give yourself a chance.

When you're about to face a television interview, 'live' or recorded, don't let arrogance or indolence get in the way of giving the best performance of which you're capable – to enable you to 'cash that cheque' we've discussed already. Don't fool yourself into thinking that your great brain and charming personality will see you through anything the professionals can throw at you, without your needing to make a serious effort of preparation. Without maximum effort on your part, it won't be 'all right on the night'. More likely, it will be a disaster that you may rue for ever after.

I've already stressed the most important factor of all – having the right *attitude* to what's ahead of you. Welcoming the opportunity. Determining to make it pay dividends. We've also discussed the need for doing your homework – listing the likely questions, your answers to them, and the way to turn them to your promotional advantage.

Now let's consider personal preparation.

First, dress. This calls for especial care, because it provides the viewer with first and last impressions.

At what time of day or night is the programme being transmitted? Who are the target audience? How does the presenter usually dress – casually or formally?

Your attire reflects not only your own personality but also the

## MAKING THE MOST OF THE MEDIA

image of your company. If you're the chief executive or a senior director/manager, you will normally appear in your smart working outfit – but if you're to be interviewed by young people on a late-night sports or entertainment programme, the formal suit will be disastrously out of place. At the same time, you don't want to give the impression of being 'mutton dressed as lamb' by wearing something that glaringly belies your age.

There may also be technical considerations. Take advice on these from the production assistant who is making the arrangements for your appearance. Almost always, the advice will be to avoid small checks: even with the most modern cameras, they have the effect of 'dancing', or strobing on the screen.

You may be asked to avoid wearing any clothing with bright blue in its patterning. This will be because of a technique known as colour separation overlay, or Chromakey. Crudely explained, this is a method by which electronic cameras are programmed to accept secondary pictures overlaid on any areas of blue. Thus, in the studio you may see a panel of plain cobalt blue on the wall behind the presenter. What the viewer at home sees is another picture, which has been fed into that space by another camera. The presenter may say: 'In Paris today ...' and in that space a picture of the Eiffel Tower appears on domestic screens. If your shirt or blouse is blue, the Eiffel Tower will appear there, too! I've explained that (in the most unscientific way possible) to allay your fears and suspicions: being asked to avoid a dress colour is by no means a hint of some political stance or other skulduggery to be adopted by the programme producers.

You may even be able to put what you wear to good promotional use. Even in formal wear, for instance, you may wear a company tie, or brooch, which will gently proclaim your company's image. If the programme is much more informal, with T-shirts or similar gear the accepted wear, there are even more legitimate ways of getting your commercial message across.

Personal grooming is clearly important – always remembering that the way you look is the way your business appears to the viewer. If your hair is lank and unwashed or uncombed; if your five o'clock shadow is obtrusive; if your make-up clearly needs freshening-up ... in short, if you look as though you have paid

## TELEVISION ... THE ART OF PERSUASION ... AND PROJECTION

little attention to your appearance, then viewers will register (possibly subconsciously, but nevertheless crucially) an impression of you and your business which is second-rate.

Make sure you leave plenty of time to reach the studio well before transmission. The last thing you want is to arrive late, working yourself up into a fine lather of nerves as a consequence. (I never can understand why some people have a problem giving themselves even a few minutes' extra time on these occasions.)

Arriving early will also provide valuable time to allow you to see the studio script and check that you're happy with the way you will be described when you are introduced. (There's nothing more likely to get an interview off to a bad start than your having to prepare your first answer with something like: 'Could I first ask you to correct what you've just said about me? I'm not the chairman, I'm the marketing director!')

There should also be a chance for you to find out the name and description it's proposed to superimpose at the bottom of the screen when you first appear – and to correct it if it's wrong, or to try to persuade the producer to 'add value' by inserting, say, your company name. You may not succeed, but it's worth a try!

Although I keep emphasising the need for a positive attitude, there is no doubt that you'll be nervous. One of the consequences for many people is to reach for 'support' – in the form of a pill or a shot of alcohol. Resist the temptation! Drugs, in whatever form, will have a bad effect on your mental agility, and even on the sharpness of your speech, when you're facing the cameras.

Television interviewers have varying techniques and you will need to respond to them. Some, for example, like to rehearse beforehand and will therefore ask you to arrive at the studio an hour or so before transmission. This may have the advantage for both of you in that both questions and answers can be unsurprising and well practised. But my own view is that this leads to less entertaining television, less spontaneity, less likelihood of revealing unexpected angles to an issue.

There's a further peril. When you're actually on air and a question is asked, it is all too easy to panic in the middle of an answer. (Have I said this already or was that in the hospitality room when we were rehearsing?) Or you may have composed a particularly apposite answer in rehearsal and become confused or tongue-tied as you struggle to reconstruct it in the studio.

Whatever the interviewer's way of working, there's one rule you should always observe: ask beforehand what the first question is going to be. Obviously, this is to give yourself time to think about your opening answer – possibly the most vital factor in your whole 'performance'.

It should persuade the viewers that this is going to be something worth watching. (There isn't much point in the exercise if bored viewers go to sleep or switch off or go into the kitchen to make a cup of tea!)

Even more important is the effect a strong start will have on you. It will give you the confidence that's an essential ingredient of a good performance. If, instead, you make a halting start, confidence will drain away and nerves will seriously damage the way you tackle the rest of the interview. (It should also be said that if you look nervous and unsure, viewers may well interpret your manner as damaging defensiveness. You look like you've something to hide!)

Although you have made many notes in the homework back at the office – which we've already described – do not under any circumstances go into the studio with them. What will almost certainly happen if you do, is that right at the start you will look down at them, rather like clinging to a lifebelt, and you won't be able to drag your eyes from them for the rest of the interview. Eyes, as I'll be emphasising later, are a key element in your armoury and a three or four-minute item during which you never look up at the interviewer will give a very poor impression.

However, you do need some kind of lifebelt! Any professional, however long in the tooth, will tell you that there come times in 'live' broadcasting when even the simplest facts are forgotten and there's that dreaded experience like a great black curtain coming across your memory. The most familiar name will suddenly be lost. More commonly, in my own experience, is a confusion of what ought to be well-remembered numbers. Did the Chancellor aim to save two million pounds – or two billion? Or was it two hundred

## TELEVISION ... THE ART OF PERSUASION ... AND PROJECTION

million? I promise you, memory lapses as huge as that are all too frequently experienced!

So without a sheaf of notes, what are you to do? I suggest you arm yourself with a small card – small enough to secrete in the palm of your hand, perhaps – on which you jot down three or four basic facts which you expect to use in the discussion or interview. You hope not to even glance at the card. But you know it's there ...

Let's return for a moment to that first question. Under any circumstances, Bill the interviewer must know what it's going to be and there is no possible reason for him to refuse your request to hear it in advance. But neither you nor he should know what the second question is going to be! This is not because he's going to try to catch you out. It's because his question ought to flow from your opening answer.

And therein lies a clue to your making the most of your opportunity. If you answer the question straightforwardly and add an extra piece of information, or inject a fresh *relevant* opinion, Bill is likely to base his next question on what you've told him. (Otherwise it may seem that he is not listening.) You are then well on your way to influencing the course of the interview and the message that you want to promote.

*But that approach will only be effective if you truly answer the original question!* You will irritate viewers and lose any good relationship with the interviewer if you try the politicians' methods. You know the sort of thing:

'Minister, how do you explain this month's serious rise in the level of unemployment?'

'Ah, Bill, before I answer that let me tell you about our success in encouraging industrial investment so far this year ...'

Sadly, politicians are almost expected to behave like that nowadays. You should not copy them!

On the studio desk there will probably be a glass of water for you. When you begin to speak, it will be natural for your mouth to dry – but I don't recommend sipping the water for relief. For me at any rate, water works only briefly and it's necessary to keep on sipping it. Resist it and the natural saliva returns permanently after that first nervous sentence or two.

Mind you, tips to combat nervousness are intensely personal and it's necessary for each individual to experiment with different methods of relaxing. Probably the most commonly effective aid is to take a number of deep breaths before performing. (There's probably a sound medical reason for this – like increasing the oxygen supply to the brain. But whatever the reason, it does work!)

I have a habit of exercising my mouth muscles, working the lips in and out. The neck is a source of tension, too, so exercising it can further aid relaxation.

We are, however, approaching difficult ground here – because, just as I recommend a *relaxed air* I must emphasise that performing at your best entails *intense concentration*. The two may seem contradictory, but they need to be combined. I suppose a sportsman provides a good example of what I'm trying to explain. A top professional golfer, for example, spends his waking life perfecting the twin skills of a totally relaxed swing – and complete concentration on guiding the clubhead through the ball.

Posture – the way you sit or stand – has the effect of helping both relaxation and concentration, with the added bonus, if practised properly, of improving the overall 'image' of the interviewee. What is often called 'body language' can often say more than words.

Above all, the eyes have it!

One of the problems usually facing novices when they go into a television studio is that the cameras act as a kind of magnet for their eyes. When you face an interviewer, there will almost certainly be a camera pointing at you from over his shoulder. You will, of course, be very conscious of it – particularly when a little red light comes on above the lens. Your eyes will be drawn away from the interviewer. Worst of all, you will nervously glance to and fro between camera and interviewer. And that will do your image no good at all.

'Shifty-eyed one, that,' viewers will comment throughout the land. 'Looks more like a sales rep for second-hand cars.'

## TELEVISION ... THE ART OF PERSUASION ... AND PROJECTION

So don't let the camera distract your honest, steady gaze.

Equally powerful is the effect of a smile. (That applies in equal measure to radio, as we shall see.) There is nothing more likely to commend you to the viewer than the warmth of a smile. You are not, of course, expected to be beaming from ear to ear if the topic being discussed is a sad or tragic one – but there are very few occasions when there isn't a place for a smile – even if it's only in the fleeting first moment of saying 'good evening'! It is, need I add, a great deal easier to smile if you have achieved that state of relaxation mentioned above.

What are you to do with your hands? That is probably the most frequent question asked by beginners. My answer is that there must not be a hard and fast rule – because we should be as natural as possible and we all have different ways with our hands in normal circumstances. There are, however, some 'hand signals' to avoid.

Some people (like me!) use their hands a great deal to emphasise what they're saying. That's fine – indeed, it can be entertainingly expressive – unless it's overdone. I remember Professor Magnus Pyke in his heyday as a television celebrity, waving his arms about like a madly spinning windmill whenever he spoke. Well, that was his trademark and it served him well – but it would not do for the rest of us and certainly not in any serious television interview, because it would take the viewers' minds off what we were saying.

Equally distracting is the nervous habit – picking at fingernails, say, or constantly clasping and unclasping hands, or perpetually scratching the forehead.

Eyes, lips, hands, the whole body should be giving the impression of someone who is at ease with himself and eager to answer questions or contribute his point of view. Again there may seem to be a contradiction in what we seek to achieve – to display a completely relaxed posture at the same time as looking animated. But being 'relaxed' doesn't mean being half asleep slumped in a chair, and being 'animated' doesn't require jumping up and down like a cat on a hot tin roof.

My own view is that the right body language will be achieved, not by working at it in the manner of a model whose movements need to be practised, but simply by getting the mental and emotional attitude right. Concentrate on the 'three Ps' and the body language will follow without effort. Persuade. Project. Promote.

Tell yourself that the only thing which matters is to persuade the interviewer and, through him, your audience about the strength of your point of view. Are you 'getting through' to them? Moving them? Convincing them? If that's your only concern, the rest will follow. Stop worrying about the form of words you're using or the risk of 'fluffing your lines'. *Persuade*! The right words will come naturally as will the right body language. You'll find yourself leaning forwards in your chair rather than looking as though you were dodging a left hook.

Persuading will lead you to *project*. If you are in a 'real' situation of addressing a large audience assembled, say, in the company canteen, nobody needs to tell you that you need to project your voice so that the person right at the back can hear you. On television, there's no point in raising your voice: the sound engineer will merely turn down the 'pot' to maintain a technical balance. But think, nonetheless, that you are trying to project what you say through the camera and across the divide between you and all those millions watching you in their homes. Reach out to them mentally and your performance will be wonderfully enhanced.

And when you succeed in both persuading your audience and projecting your personality, use these advantages to *promote* your company or your personal message. The opportunity – the blank cheque – is there for you.

Cash it!

## CHAPTER EIGHT

# Radio ... the missing dimension ... and the need for colour

Working on radio is in several ways more challenging than appearing on television.

There are, of course, some aspects of personal appearance that may seem to call for less care. Combing your hair or dressing smartly may not seem to matter (unless the programme is broadcast in front of an audience) though I'm not so sure about that. Feeling smart and well-groomed can actually add a degree of confidence and ease which will be reflected in the way you speak.

The voice reflects so much – and, clearly, the voice is the thing that's going to provide listeners with the clue to your personality.

I wrote earlier that a smile is important on radio. How? Well, think of the last programme you listened to: I'm sure you knew when speakers were smiling, even though you couldn't see them. Their smiles added colour to their voices. And it's colour, or if you like light and shade, which we need to develop if we're to overcome radio's missing dimension – pictures.

In normal social conversation, we all add colour, in varying degrees, to the way we speak. Very simply, we'll 'punch' the key word or phrase in spoken sentences, or slow the pace of our speech to add emphasis to the point we're making ... and then rattle through a few phrases which are no more than bridges to the next key statement we want to emphasise.

Not only will the pace of the way we speak vary. So will the tone of voice.

This varying colour is an essential part of being 'entertaining' and holding the attention of those listening. At home, in the pub or at work, all that comes naturally. In the radio studio it doesn't!

As with television studio paraphernalia, so the microphones and acoustic trappings of radio somehow have the effect of making us lapse into formal, 'written' English. We're even more likely to do that, of course, if we actually have written words in front of us. A handful of great actors can read a script and make it sound as though it is ad lib, unprepared. The rest of us can't.

There's another challenge to the radio performer that comes from the missing dimension: silence is death!

If you're lost for a phrase when appearing on television, it's actually interesting (even eliciting sympathy among viewers) to watch you pausing and looking – heavenwards! – in search of the words you need. On radio, the thunderous silence merely makes the listener wonder whether the station has gone off air and adds critically to your own nervousness. So it may be said that radio creates more tension than television and requires even more thorough mental and physical preparation beforehand.

On that note, two examples from my own experience ...

For five years I was chairman of radio's long-running (already more than 30 years in my time) weekly programme, *Gardeners' Question Time*. And it might be argued that its success could be at least in part attributable to a pair of socks and a bar of chocolate.

The three members of my team were Fred Loads from Lancaster, Bill Sowerbutts from Ashton-under-Lyne and Scotsman Alan Gemmell from Keele University. I soon learned that to ensure a successful recording with 'the lads' at their best, my job had little to do with presentational skills on air. Much more important was to see that they had their home comforts beforehand. We used to travel the length and breadth of the country, often visiting remote hamlets and staying over Saturday nights in a local hotel.

When Patricia, the programme assistant, made the hotel booking, only one thing mattered: did it have a television set? If not, we couldn't stay there – because Alan had to be able to watch

# RADIO ... THE MISSING DIMENSION ... AND THE NEED FOR COLOUR

*Match of the Day*. Otherwise, he'd be decidedly out of form come recording time next day.

Then there was the matter of Bill's socks. He suffered from cold feet in bed, so we had to make sure he'd brought a pair of long woolly socks with him.

And the bar of chocolate? Fred suffered from a novel form of night starvation which meant that he always woke up in the early hours craving chocolate. If there was a bar beside the bed, he'd scoff it and float back into a satisfied sleep which would ensure a lively performance from him next day.

Even when we arrived at the village hall for recording, preparation had little to do with the job in hand. The sound engineers would want to test the balance of our microphones and Ken Ford the producer would want to 'warm up' the audience at the same time, so the lads would each have to tell a funny story. Now that led to serious discussion before we went 'on stage'. Could Alan tell the one about the cannibal and the naked girl in the jungle? Patricia would peer into the hall from our backstage room and tell us whether the vicar was there – or perhaps some fierce be-hatted ladies who might object. Not today, Alan! Mind you, it was difficult to prevent Bill telling the one about the woman of ill repute who walked into a pub carrying a canary in a cage.

'I'm prepared,' she announced, 'to sleep with anyone who can tell me the correct weight of this canary.'

'Twenty-eight pounds,' yelled a wag at the bar.

'C'mon, it's near enough.'

Yes, I should remind you that all this was in aid of *Gardeners' Question Time*, not *Radio Music Hall*.

Perhaps it was an extreme example, but it surely made the point that you're likely to perform better at any level if you work hard beforehand at getting 'in the mood'.

Another example was *Any Questions?* on which I was often a panellist in the days when David Jacobs was in the chair. It was then, as it has always been, a 'live' show in which we had no notice whatsoever of the questions to be put to us from members of the audience.

So how could we prepare ourselves to give of our best? Well, producer Michael Bowen would ask us to assemble in the local hotel for afternoon tea (very Auntie BBC-ish!) to get to know each other – for me, at any rate, a vital exercise because some of the panel members would be people of great eminence, which didn't help the pre-programme butterflies. Then Michael would leaf through the pages of the *Daily Telegraph* looking for stories which he thought might prove to be the subject of questions. If any of us had missed a particular story in the week's news, this helped us to do at least some superficial homework so that we wouldn't be entirely 'thrown' by an unexpected question about which we were entirely ignorant.

This session would be followed by dinner when conversation on topical issues ranged far and wide and we developed something of a team spirit together.

In the event, of course, we were still caught out by unexpected questions (when we'd each try to avoid David's eye and pray that one of the others would be asked to answer first). But there is no doubt that the careful preparation was essential to the quality of performance.

One last word about *Any Questions*? A few days after its transmission, we would each be sent a typed transcript of the programme. Despite the fact that members of the team were often masters of the English language (humbling for me) there would be *hardly a grammatical sentence to be found*! To hear, it might be a wonderful example of lucidity and literacy. To read, it sometimes seemed like gobbleydegook.

See what I mean about two languages?

I suppose it could be said that radio is the poor relation of the broadcasters and there's no doubt that its budgets are minuscule compared with big brother TV. (I once put it to the managing director of BBC Radio at the time, the late Sir Ian Trethowan, that it was astonishing how many professionals were prepared to work for radio considering the tiny fees offered. 'I agree,' he said. 'In effect they're working for charity.')

Yet radio has grown in stature in recent years. With all the local stations added to the national networks, there's a substantial

# RADIO ... THE MISSING DIMENSION ... AND THE NEED FOR COLOUR

audience each day – and a 'committed' one. So it's well worth courting. If your message is one that targets community audiences, it is certainly the broadcast medium for you.

Radio programmes are, of course, particularly fond of the phone-in (ideal for low budgets!) so be prepared to respond to calls at any time – at home or at work, sometimes even in the car.

Opportunity may knock today. Are you ready?

## CHAPTER NINE

# The press ... a question of ethics ... off-the-record dangers and opportunities

My main message, that the media provide individuals and businesses with rich promotional pickings, is perhaps hardest to sustain when we enter the world of newspapers and magazines. It still holds – but, my goodness, what awful pitfalls await the unwary.

To a large extent, this may be due to the decline in standards of both ethics and professional competence in recent years. I'm now going to sound rather old (yes, policemen do seem extraordinarily young these days!) but I have to say that press people are not what they used to be.

In days gone by when I first entered the profession, there was much criticism of the lack of formal education required to become a journalist. In the popular papers at least, university degrees were rare among entrants. School records, I suppose, had some influence in the recruitment process but the only qualifications demanded of me at the age of 16 were certificates in shorthand (120 words a minute) and typing (70). Neither the proprietors nor the unions had any formal kind of certification.

And yet the 'hands-on' training was vigorous to the point of ruthlessness. A cub reporter sent to a funeral and required to list the names of 100 or so mourners was liable to lose his job if a name was misspelt or initials wrongly recorded. The shorthand notebook needed to be reliable enough to be used as evidence in a court of law.

Unbending insistence on the really basic skills was matched by a high degree of moral integrity. Quite simply, confidences accepted were never broken. All the dirty tricks of the game today would have resulted in a reporter's sacking if used then. It wasn't namby-pamby journalism by any stretch of the imagination – we were a tough bunch with a burning determination to seek truth and expose wrongs – but strict ethics ruled our working lives.

Today, the newspaper world has changed dramatically (it's rare to find a reporter who can write shorthand) and the way you respond to its opportunities for promoting yourself or your business needs very careful study. It's not in my nature to deal in negatives, but in this area there are sadly quite a few. For example:

- *Don't* give any journalist a piece of information 'in confidence' – unless you actually want him to publish it. (Quite seriously, there are many political spin doctors who advise their clients to ensure publication of a fact or a viewpoint by 'letting slip' some titbit 'strictly confidentially and not for publication, of course'.)

- *Don't* be fooled by the reporter ostentatiously putting away notebook or tape recorder on the pretext that what you say thereafter will be 'not for publication, of course – just to ensure I don't get the story wrong'.

- *Don't* give a formal 'feature' interview without taking the precaution of recording everything that's said on your own equipment. You will probably be misquoted in the printed piece, but at least you will have some redress (legal, if the misrepresentation is serious) if you have proof of what actually transpired.

- *Don't* be tricked into refusing to comment in circumstances where a line like 'Mrs Bloggs refused to answer questions' in a report could leave a damaging impression. Instead, sound helpful but firm. For instance: 'I can't talk right now because I'm with a client but I'll call you back in an hour.' That also buys you time to think about the issue and compose your reactions.

## OFF-THE-RECORD DANGERS AND OPPORTUNITIES

- *Don't* lose your temper – even if the reporter is rude. You may say things you'll later regret and the reporter will be given the impression that you're rattled because there's something to hide.

However, having posted all those warnings I can still advise that co-operation with the press may bring dividends. Maybe I should provide an example in my personal – very personal! – experience where my cynicism and distrust of the 'rat pack' taught me the lesson that openness will often be the best policy.

When I was the presenter of *Nationwide* – a family show in the early evening, remember – my marriage foundered. They were difficult days and it wasn't easy to appear on screen night after night with a relaxed smile on my face. It also seemed to me that a very public 'celebrity divorce' would not be too good for the image of the programme. So I went to great lengths to avoid publicity and hide the facts from my friends in the press. I told the programme editor in confidence but otherwise not even my close colleagues knew. And I managed (with my wife's co-operation, of course) to pursue the legal proceedings through an obscure local courtroom.

It worked. Not a word got out.

And then, a year or so later, Dilys Morgan joined the team of studio presenters. Some months afterwards we fell in love and – still hidden from public gaze – began to live together.

The first story to break was in the *Daily Mirror* which ran it under a great splash headline: 'Secret divorce for Barratt of *Nationwide*'. And then I realised that my 'clever' suppression of my marriage break-up was not too clever after all ... for the headline ran atop a huge photograph of Dilys and the story included this paragraph: 'Last night 28-year-old Dilys Morgan, who works alongside Mr Barratt as an interviewer on *Nationwide*, declined to discuss her friendship with him.'

And then the chase really began! Nigel Dempster of the *Daily Mail*, with whom I've since worked on several happy assignments, led his famous Diary with a story headed: 'Why they say, nationwide, that Mike and Dilys have wed'.

'They' were wrong – I had certainly not married my 'constant companion'. And the last titbit in Nigel's story carried a ludicrous insinuation. 'One touch about Mr Barratt's office relationship with Dilys I rather like is his habit of communicating in the studio with her by note – passed over the desk.' If I ever did pass a note across, it certainly didn't say anything like 'I love you' but more likely, 'Don't forget you're on camera 3 for the next intro.'

(I discovered later that the gossip about our 'working relationship' had actually been passed to Nigel by a BBC press officer for a reward of £25. It's not only the journalists who abandon professional ethics: beware of your own colleagues.)

For the next year, until we did marry – in the Caribbean to escape the fuss – Dilys and I were followed and photographed almost everywhere we went. And the implication in all the stories was that she was the 'scarlet woman' who had enticed me away from my loving wife and family. In fact, as I've explained, we had never clapped eyes on each other when my divorce proceedings began: it was my attempt to hide the original story from the press that led to this misinterpretation of the facts which was so unfairly hurtful to Dilys.

So if you're in the public eye, don't kid yourself that you can select the newsworthy stories about you or your business which the papers will publish. If you try to be too clever and manipulative (as I was) then the consequences may be more than you bargained for.

And it's pointless to complain that your private life is your own. It isn't any more. Anyway, it has always been my view that those of us who seek high-profile success in any sphere – politics, business, entertainment, whatever – must accept the constantly searching spotlight of publicity in the same way that we strive for high rewards.

So how are you to nurture good relations with the press, on the one hand avoiding all the pitfalls I've mentioned but on the other seeking valuable promotional chances?

First of all, you can take – and make – every opportunity to meet them and feed them with 'good stories' (see my chapter on PR). Then you can develop personal relationships that make you of more value to them as a friend and source of information than as a target for what's known in the trade as 'knocking copy'.

I've always regarded my good friend Jimmy Hill the football

## OFF-THE-RECORD DANGERS AND OPPORTUNITIES

pundit as a shining example. With a domestic background which is, to put it mildly, at least as colourful as my own, he has never attracted a hint of gossip in the tabloids. In the days when we worked together on *Nationwide,* I used to be baffled by the way he seemed to escape the kind of gossip-mongering 'going-over' that was my fate ... until I observed him handling the Fleet Street pack with easy skill. The lads invited to join him for breakfast in his London home were most unlikely to bite the hand that fed them precious sports gossip along with their bacon and eggs!

But again a strong word of caution. (I seem to be blowing hot and cold on this question of press relations.) Sir Bernard Ingham, one of our most outstanding journalists – who has turned into a kind of PR guru – has written: 'What sheltered lives are led by Britain's top managers outside politics. Most of them are unfit to be allowed anywhere near the media jungle lest they be eaten alive.'

Put it another way: if you want to make the most of press publicity, you almost certainly have a great deal to learn. If you're not prepared to devote real time and effort to the learning, find yourself a professional adviser.

You know by now how high the stakes are!

Let's now look a trifle more prosaically at some of the ways in which you and your company colleagues can co-operate with newspapers and magazines to mutual advantage.

First, remember that newspapers have deadlines which are likely to be rather more pressing than any you're used to. Working on a story, they often have no more than an hour or two to complete it. Even in these days of high technology computerised printing, the early editions of the morning papers may be 'put to bed' early the previous evening to catch trains or planes or lorries distributing them to remote locations. So if a reporter calls you to ask for information which you don't have immediately to hand, he may ask you to call him back 'in ten minutes, please'. And he means it! Fail him and you may miss the chance of a valuable 'mention' for your company.

Even publications which are only produced monthly or quarterly may have 'long lead times' – which means that they go to the printer's a month or more before they appear on the bookstalls or news-stands. The pressure of a deadline is still there –

MAKING THE MOST OF THE MEDIA

and the need for you to respond swiftly (or publish your press release early enough) is just as great.

If you're meeting a journalist for a sustained chat, the much-maligned lunch may be an effective and relaxed way of feeding him information – but don't let your guard down by drinking too much, and don't run away with the idea that, if you're paying the bill, he feels any kind of obligation to praise you in print! Before lunch, do your homework by looking at previous issues of his journal to get a feeling for its style; finding out what you can about him and his attitudes; making sure you're well 'boned-up' on the subject in question and your company's policy stance. That way you're more likely to be able to interest him in your promotional line.

A specialised journalist within your commercial or professional work sector may ask you to give him a 'background briefing' on some topic to give the piece he's writing added authority. Always bearing in mind the cautionary notes at the beginning of this chapter, such briefings can be extremely valuable even if the published article makes no mention of you or your company. They may be the beginning of a relationship in which you become well regarded by the journal and so in a strong position to influence its writings in the future to your firm's or your own personal advantage. (An inch of promotion in the editorial columns may be worth much more than a paid-for advertisement!)

For the more popular press in particular, 'think headlines' when you're facing a reporter with a notebook. This might be called the printed equivalent of radio and TV's 'soundbite'. If you've dreamed up a pithy phrase before meeting, it has a good chance of being seized upon for the story that eventually gets into print.

Never say 'no comment' to a reporter! There's no knowing what he can do with that ...

'Did you beat your wife this morning?'
'No comment.'

'Is it true that your company is having cashflow difficulties?'
'No comment.'

'Why did your managing director retire early?'
'No comment.'

## OFF-THE-RECORD DANGERS AND OPPORTUNITIES

The implications in instances like that are capable of sounding far worse than the truth!

Sometimes, of course, you will not know the answer to a question. In that case, don't waffle or bluster – simply admit you don't know and if possible promise to find out.

Develop a reputation for being helpful to the press and you're more likely to end up on the 'good news' pages.

## CHAPTER TEN

# The professionals who aren't professional ... and the way to turn the tables

Honor Blackman, one of our finest actresses, was most celebrated, at one time in her career, for her role as Cathie Gale, the stunningly attractive exponent of the arts of self-defence in the television series *The Avengers*.

One evening, she was booked to appear in a regional TV current affairs magazine programme. She arrived in the green room before transmission and met the show's presenter who was about to interview her. Now Honor is a particularly delightful woman, courteous and, of course, professional to her fingertips. Her interviewer was relatively unknown except in his own patch where he was conscious of being a 'star'.

'Would you like to go through any of the questions you want to ask me beforehand?' asked Honor, trying to be helpful.

'Oh no, I never rehearse *my* interviews,' he replied with an arrogant air which was hardly calculated to endear him to the real star of this pair.

In the studio on transmission, he opened the interview with a question delivered in his most supercilious and offensive manner: 'Honor Blackman, best known as the leather-clad Avenger, what does it feel like to be half man, half woman?'

Honor was wearing a low-cut dress and leaned over towards

him, checking as she did so in the monitor screen on the studio floor that there was plenty on view.

'I don't quite understand the question,' she said. 'Which half are you talking about?'

It was, effectively, the end of any kind of rapport between insensitive interviewer and his so-professional guest.

Not many of us can claim the quick wit or (when goaded) lethal charm of Miss Blackman. But that story does embrace several lessons worth learning.

First of all, you are not always going to be favoured with an experienced and well-skilled interviewer. There are plenty of baddies around! (This probably emanates from the huge proliferation of regional and local TV and radio stations in recent years. The supply of first-class reporters and interviewers is naturally limited – and the lack of financial resources of many small broadcasting organisations means they do not have the facilities to provide thorough training.)

If you are faced with an incompetent or unnecessarily aggressive interviewer, remember that it's not your job to protect him or her. If the question is badly phrased and so woolly that you don't understand it, say so. Don't try to be helpful by answering what you think may be the drift of the question. Politely, you say: 'I'm sorry, I don't quite understand what you're asking me. Would you mind putting it another way?'

One form of lazy question is the one that jumbles up several: 'Why aren't your company's drugs tested for a longer period, if not on humans then at least on animals, to determine if there may be harmful side-effects, and that being so how do you justify the cost – especially as you claim to support the National Health Service?'

I am not joking. It is not uncommon for questions as long-winded and confusing as that to be asked by my less talented brethren. But in a way, they're a gift to be eagerly accepted – because they allow you to respond courteously with a smile: 'Well, you've asked me rather a lot of questions there. So let me first answer the one about ...' and you gratefully pick the issue on which you *want* to develop your own case.

Then there is the irritating arrogance of the second-rate interviewers who consider themselves 'stars' (in a way the real

## THE PROFESSIONALS WHO AREN'T PROFESSIONAL

pros rarely do) and delight in asking questions which are designed to exhibit their own cleverness rather than elicit interesting answers from you. This attitude also leads them more often than not into unnecessary and unattractive aggression. They think their role is to try to trip you up and leave you begging for their mercy while they imagine they're earning the plaudits of their 'fans' watching or listening at home.

It is fairly easy to cope with these people. The simplest ruse of all is to give them one-word answers. A straight yes or no as often as not will throw them off their stride. In no time at all they'll be reduced to hesitant inadequacy as they frantically search their notepads for another question to keep the interview alive.

The best kind of interview, as I've already indicated, is achieved when interviewer and guest strike up an intelligent rapport – however controversial the topic may be. But if that is not to be, remember that you normally have a significant advantage in being more knowledgeable than your questioner.

Consider another facet of the way a programme is put together. The editor says to one of his team: 'Mary, I'd like you to tackle the item on bread. Prices have been put up by the leading bakers today and there are already complaints from customers that the quality of bread is declining as its price rises. What's the industry's response?'

Now Mary already has a couple of other subjects to tackle in the programme this evening – a fishing dispute in offshore waters and a political row over pensions. She glances at the clock to confirm her worst fears that there's only an hour left to transmission and hurriedly calls up the 'news information library' in another part of the building, asking someone there to send over 'the file on bread'. When it arrives, she will have minutes only to riffle through the newspaper cuttings it contains. They will give her at best a skimpy background to the problems of the baking industry. Worse, some of the stories will be inaccurate and even distorted.

Let's say you're a master baker, brought into the studio to be questioned by Mary. Even if she attempts to grill you and accuse you and your colleagues of sharp practice, she does so from a most vulnerable position. *You* are the expert with a lifetime's experience at your fingertips. She is working from the scantiest of knowledge.

So provided you keep your head, remain courteous, and respond with convincing facts that are also informative, you should be able to hold your own – and then proceed to 'cash that cheque' – however tough the questions.

Just one word of warning, though. You must never *assume* ignorance on the part of the interviewer and consequently try to get away with smug answers that are not strictly true. It's just possible that Mary's father is a baker, or that a researcher has been helping her to prepare the interview with some very sound background information. In that case, your too-clever answers will be exposed and you will destroy the credibility of the whole of your performance.

So far, the examples I have given of studio interviews have been based on 'live' radio or television. Unhappily, that's becoming ever rarer these days – in TV at any rate – and the trend towards more recorded items presents perils of a different kind.

Bluntly stated, recorded interviews, edited back at the studios before transmission, may frequently be distorted – though not necessarily deliberately. If a reporter dashes back to his office with a 20-minute interview that needs to be cut to two minutes' duration – and if the tape editor has, say, no more than half an hour to finish the job before transmission time – then the chances of the finished piece being a fair reflection of the original are practically nil.

How is that to be avoided? I suggest that when a programme assistant rings to ask you to record an interview in your office, you firstly ascertain whether it's possible instead to do it 'live'. (Unlike newspapers, in which your words can so easily be misreported, in 'live' radio or TV the words really are your words, emanating from your mouth and unalterable.)

However, this may not be possible. So when the reporter comes to the office, the conversation should run something like this:

*You*: 'How long do you intend the piece to be when it's transmitted tonight?'

*Reporter*: 'Oh, don't worry about that. We can record as much as we like – several "takes" if necessary – so there's no need to worry about time.'

## THE PROFESSIONALS WHO AREN'T PROFESSIONAL

*You*: 'Yes, but it would help me enormously if I could know the length you need – help me to concentrate my mind and try to be as succinct as I can. I'm terribly long-winded given half a chance! Maybe if we treated it as a "live" interview it would work better. I'd be very grateful ...'

You are being courteous, even self-effacing – but at the same time (without actually saying so!) trying to prevent distortion in editing.

Incidentally it's also vital that before agreeing to a recording you establish exactly how it is going to be used in the ultimate programme. If there is a danger that what you say will be sliced into sections (or soundbites as they've come to be known) and 'intercut' with other unspecified people, beware. Unless you are perfectly happy that the method to be adopted will not distort your message, decline the invitation.

None of these tips will help you, of course, if you are the target of the new media's 'foot-in-the-door' reporting. It is quite common now for a business executive, say, to be telephoned (perhaps as he's driving to work) by a radio or TV station as it transmits its programme. They want an immediate, off-the-cuff comment about an issue of the day or perhaps about the executive's own personal or business affairs. That really does call for quick thinking! It also underlines the need for everybody in responsible positions in business to be trained and prepared for out-of-the-blue interrogation any time, any day. But there is one safeguard: your caller will not be the programme presenter on air; it will be an assistant who asks if you are prepared to talk ('I'll put you through to our presenter if you're happy'). So even in such 'instant-access' circumstances, you can still say no!

But after you have digested the message of this book, that's a word you'll be most reluctant to use ...

CHAPTER ELEVEN

• • • • • • • • • • • • • • • •

## Crisis! . . . preparing for the worst

The call came to me from a major PR company: 'We have a client, Zero Foods [I've changed the name], who have just come close to a disaster which could have ruined them if the media had got hold of the facts. It has made them realise the urgent need for training. Can you help?'

When I heard the story, I realised they needed much more than straightforward training in how to face the media: they were prime candidates for the full crisis management treatment.

The facts of the case were that a hotel had complained that a glass jar containing their sauce had been found to contain a sliver of glass, which seemed to have broken off the neck of the jar. Fortunately, it was spotted before the hotel's guest might have swallowed it – with alarming consequences.

With commendable speed, the production director of Zero Foods stopped the relevant production line to try to determine whether there might be a problem during the filling process. To his alarm, he discovered that 2 per cent of the jars that had been delivered in a recent batch were faulty.

Now this could certainly be categorised as potentially life-threatening. What was the company to do? Stop further production of that batch, of course. Call back all jars from the hotel, naturally. But would that be enough – either morally or commercially? What if the media got wind of the story? With only one incident reported, there was a chance that it might not get out – but if *all* jars were recalled from both commercial and domestic

## MAKING THE MOST OF THE MEDIA

customers nationwide (which was arguably the only ethical course) the story certainly would reach the media's ears and the company could be in serious trouble.

Clearly a decision had to be made speedily and at the highest level: after all, millions of pounds and even the company's future were at stake. However, the chief executive was abroad and the rest of the board were not prepared to take such a decision without him. They called him by phone and explained all the facts that had so far come to light.

He decided to take a risk. No more production off this line until a new batch of jars, fully quality-tested, had been delivered to the factory. But no nationwide recall. It was a case of heads down, fingers crossed, hope the problem will go away with no further 'accidents'.

I still feel a shiver down the spine when I remember that case and ponder what might have been. If there had been another incident – perhaps even a fatal one – and the media then discovered (as they would) that Zero Foods had knowingly left suspect jars in general use instead of recalling them or even warning customers of the dangers ... well, the consequences hardly bear thinking about.

As it happened, the company's luck held. But the whole affair jolted them into the realisation that they must have a proper strategy in place to cope with any crisis in the future. Training a team of company spokespeople to face media questioning was clearly a necessity – but much more needed to be done, like establishing a crisis management team at the ready, round the clock, 365 days a year, to respond to any kind of emergency in a pre-arranged, well-rehearsed manner.

The number of crises that can happen to companies and individuals are almost countless: they may not be anybody's fault (like acts of God) nor may they be predictable (like acts of terror). But we *can* prepare for them – and it surely makes sense to spend a thousand or two on professional preparation if it is to insure ourselves or our companies against crises that could cost billions if mishandled.

Case histories which teach us all lessons frequently occur. I think that without exception they underline the enormous power of the media which really can make the difference between corporate life or death.

My friend Mike Hopkins, a director of Nabisco UK before the famous Leveraged Buy-Out, had first-hand experience of crises like a disgruntled machine operator's malicious tampering with the contents of crisp packets, and often cites the stories of Tylenol and the Piper Alpha oil rig tragedy.

Johnson & Johnson's Tylenol is one of the best-known painkillers in the United States. In September 1982, seven people in the Chicago area died after taking Tylenol capsules. It was found that the capsules contained cyanide. Tests showed that 75 capsules, all in one batch, had been contaminated – out of eight million. It was clearly established that the lethal tampering had occurred only in the Chicago area. Nevertheless, Johnson & Johnson took the decision to recall all stock throughout the USA. That cost them millions of dollars. They also spent half a million dollars to alert doctors about what had happened.

From the moment the original tragic news broke, the media were hot in pursuit. More than 2 500 calls were logged from the press, radio and television. Disaster for the company? No, opportunity! I wouldn't be so callous as to suggest that they profited from people's deaths – of course not – but they quite properly persuaded the media that they deserved admiration and support for the steps they had taken. They were widely quoted for their company policy which every employee is exhorted to observe – that their first concern must be for its public and customers. And there was high praise for the company chairman who was conspicuous throughout in being seen to take the public-spirited decisions whatever the cost. He was permanently available to the media and gave many interviews almost every day.

Johnson & Johnson's final move was to develop a tamper-proof pack for their capsules – and to halt production entirely until the pack had been perfected.

The media applauded. And the company restored their share of the market – a massive 35 per cent with $450 million annual sales – as well as showing the way to its competitors by pioneering safe packaging.

As for Piper Alpha, this is how Mike Hopkins relates what happened:

On 6 July 1988, the public affairs manager of Occidental Oil received a simple message at home. It said: 'Fire on Piper!' Within the next 24 hours he was to learn that 167 men had died in the worst accident on an oil rig in history. Fortunately, Alex Blake Milton had a well-rehearsed crisis procedure and the crisis was meticulously handled. However, the most significant fact was that the first official visitor to the Royal Infirmary at Aberdeen where the injured were taken was Dr Armand Hammer, chairman of Occidental, who had flown in from Los Angeles. He was *followed* by the Prime Minister and the Prince and Princess of Wales. By that action, Dr Hammer demonstrated his personal concern for the victims (his employees) and their families.

It was, of course, one of the biggest media stories in years. Pages of newsprint, hours of sound and television reports were seen and heard by every person in the land. All of it reflected the image and the reputation of Occidental. And the lasting image was that of a caring man.

Mike's conclusion when he tells the story to his crisis management pupils is simple: 'There is no doubt about it, the media can make or break your company!'

One more example of my own, which I often tell when dubious businesspeople react to my exhortations for a positive attitude to the media by saying something like: 'It's all very well telling us that interviews always provide an opportunity to promote our companies, but in our experience we're only asked to appear when there's *bad* news to talk about.'

I ask them to consider the case of the building site in the Midlands where a huge crane collapsed and killed its operator. The site was being developed by one of our leading construction companies with a high reputation. On the face of it, what happened seemed to denote lax practices and a failure to observe health and safety procedures. In the studio that night, the company's site manager faced the music:

*Presenter*: 'This was a terrible tragedy. How did it happen?'

*Manager*: 'At the moment, I have no idea. All the normal

procedures seem to have been in place and we have found no structural weaknesses in the crane. However, we *will* find the reason for it. Our own technical experts are searching for clues alongside health and safety investigators at this moment and I can tell you they won't give up tonight until they've solved the mystery.'

(In a sense, more important than what he said was his demeanour. He looked grey, distraught even, clearly still traumatised by the loss of a workmate. As viewers, we could hardly be other than moved and sympathetic.)

*Presenter*: 'There have been suggestions that your safety procedures were possibly inadequate.'

*Manager*: 'That's almost impossible to imagine. My company, Bloggs Construction [name changed!] probably has the best safety record in the industry. We spent a million pounds last year alone on safety training and the latest protective equipment. We ...'

*Presenter* (interrupting): 'But that's little consolation to the dead man's family.'

*Manager*: 'Sir Peter, the company chairman, is with his wife now. He was on holiday in the South of France when he was told of the tragedy and immediately chartered a plane to bring him to support the family ...'

As the interview developed, so did viewers' sympathy with the manager and their impression of a major company, with above average safety standards, patently caring for an employee. That manager 'cashed the cheque' all right – not by PR waffle but by simply reflecting the human face of a highly reputable company.

It was said some time ago in *Business Magazine* that: 'Crisis is not always something that happens to other people – most companies will have to cope with one at some time in their history.'

So how should you prepare for a crisis? Mike Hopkins argues that there are four key actions to be taken:

1. Select a small crisis management team.
2. Establish a crisis procedure.

3. Nominate and equip incident rooms.

4. Train and rehearse!

I leave it to him to write the definitive book on crisis management and to explain the process of establishing structures like incident rooms, but let me quote his views on the topic that's the core of this book:

> I cannot emphasise strongly enough that you *must* take a positive approach to the media and see your exposure as an *opportunity* for promoting the goodwill of your company and the quality of its product or service.

He's saying what I've emphasised from the start: the key to making the most of the media – in a crisis or not – is to be found in your *attitude* to it.

## CHAPTER TWELVE

# On your own ... forward with technology ... but back to basics

Let's now look at those times when you are on your own. No professional interviewer to steer you in the right direction. No adversaries in a debate to stimulate you. Just you and your audience, seen or (as in radio and television) unseen.

How are you to give of your best? Well, most of the skills already discussed in previous pages apply, of course, but there are now other factors which come into play – in particular, the help that technology can give. Mind you, we must be careful not to allow the tail to wag the dog: allowing the wizardry of computer graphics, multimedia interaction, virtual reality and all the rest to control your performance, rather than be a slave to it, can lead to disaster.

In its simplest forms, the visual aids of overhead projection and slides can add a useful dimension to what you have to say. Yet time after time speakers misuse them.

Most common of all is the speaker who regards his slides or acetates as sufficient guarantee that his or her presentation will sustain the audience's interest. They won't. What they will do is tempt you to ignore your homework and personal preparation (audience research, logical argument, grooming and all the rest).

Cristina Stuart, as managing director of presentation company Speak Easy, once wrote (in *PR Week*) that:

No one has ever told me they chose an agency because they

liked their visual aids or thought they were a dab hand at operating a laptop. New technology – even carefully chosen and professionally used – will rarely give an agency the edge in the new business beauty parade. People who know their stuff and have been trained to show empathy, understanding and enthusiasm will always win the day.

So how are we to make the best use of visual aids? By making them our slaves! By making sure that they complement and support what we have to say.

Let me give you a real example of the wrong way to use slides in a presentation. It happened at one of those breakfast meetings that have become a feature of business life in Britain. You know the pattern: businesspeople meet at about eight in the morning in some attractive hotel room for breakfast. Towards the end of the meal, a speaker makes a relatively informal presentation which claims to be a straightforward exposition of some topical subject (the effects of the Budget, opportunities for small business development, maximising European Union aid – that sort of thing) but which usually turns out to be a fairly soft-sell promotional exercise.

On this occasion, we were to be treated to a talk on the power of visual aids. As the eating bit of the breakfast session drew to a close, we were all asked to move to another room – because the area in which we had gathered (a delightful conservatory) was too brightly sunlit for the speaker's purpose.

Reluctantly, we moved to a darkened room where a projector was placed in the aisle between rows of chairs and a rather rickety-looking screen showed the out-of-focus title of the presentation. As each guest entered the room, the screen wobbled. The speaker began by apologising for asking us to leave the breakfast tables and then flipped through a series of slides which contained misspellings in text, facts which conflicted with what he was saying and, to complete a nightmare, one slide which appeared upside down.

At first I admired this witty way of showing us all how not to use visual aids. And then I began to realise that these were not deliberate mistakes but an example of bad presentation techniques of which the speaker seemed blissfully unaware. The consequence was a feeling among the audience that the very last thing they would want to do would be to invest in visual aids for their own business presentations.

Consider the mistakes:

1. Moving people from their comfortable breakfast tables underlined the limitations of the slide technique.
2. Placing the projector on a floor which wobbled every time someone entered the room gave an amateur air to the whole presentation.
3. Showing 'soft' pictures by failing to focus the slides beforehand added to the amateur feeling.
4. Failing to check spelling displayed a lack of basic values or 'quality testing'.
5. Showing a slide upside down showed a carelessness which was a final insult to the audience.

There were that morning another couple of mistakes which are so common that they may be described as 'normal' – showing the slide too soon, and then reading every word it displays.

If a slide is to support what you want to say, then it should follow and back up your words, not anticipate them. Here's a simple example. You want to say something like:

> Now let's turn to the subject of internal communication in business.
>
> The first thing that any manager must do if he is to communicate successfully with his team is to *listen*. Take the trouble to hear what's being said on the shopfloor – whether people are anxious about the company's future, or angry because they feel they're not being properly rewarded, or unproductive because the machinery they're using is outdated, or whatever.
>
> In any of those or other circumstances, your job essentially is to *inform* them about what's going on, what steps are being taken to remedy problems, and so on.
>
> But straightforward information will not be enough. Your next step is to *motivate* them, in ways that I'll outline later ...

And so on.

If you have a visual aid on a screen beside you, it should build gradually so that it begins simply with the 'headline' 'Internal Communication'. And that should not appear on screen until you actually speak the phrase. After that, you introduce the other sub-heads (the words I've italicised above) as you voice them – not before. Eventually your screen will look like this:

INTERNAL COMMUNICATION

- Listen
- Inform
- Motivate

The whole impact of the presentation will be spoilt if you put up the whole frame at the beginning: your audience will read it instead of taking in what you are saying. They will be reading the word 'motivate', for example, while you're still exhorting them to 'listen'!

Worse still is the very common practice of displaying long sentences on screen – and then simply reading them to the audience. That's not only pointless – it's positively irritating and patronising! Does the presenter assume that the audience can't read? And if you're going to provide the speech in printed form on a screen, why bother to stand up and speak at all? Why not just hand round printed notes for the audience to read at their leisure?

Simple key words have real visual impact and help to lodge a message in the memory, adding real value to the spoken word.

I may seem to have spent a long time hammering home this very simple message, but in my experience the misuse and mistiming of visual aids is the most common fault in this type of presentation.

Almost as common – and even more basic – is the failure to ask this question before the audience gathers and the presentation begins: can I be seen and heard?

Yes, that really is simplicity taken to childlike levels – yet I'd wager that most readers of this book will have attended seminars or other gatherings where the public address system hasn't worked properly – or maybe hasn't even existed; where the speaker has been at floor level so as to be unseen by people in back rows; where the

## ON YOUR OWN...

lighting has been such that words or diagrams on screen have been unreadable; and so on. If you are the speaker in such circumstances, you will fail to make your intended impact and, indeed, may even destroy the very message you're aiming to convey. (A plea for higher quality standards in industry is likely to fall on deaf ears if the quality of the presentation itself is third-rate!)

As in other spheres of communication, you will only give of your best if you have the self-confidence that comes from thorough preparation and meticulous technical support. A voice from the back of the hall exclaiming 'Speak up, please', or a sea of heads in front of you all anxiously craning their necks to try to catch a glimpse of you is hardly inspiring.

One of the most popular aids to presenters nowadays is some form of Autocue. (I use the capital A because it's a particular company name though, like Hoover, it has become the generic term for a system offered by many other outfits – Portaprompt, Teleprompt and all the rest.)

By projecting words through reflective mirrors, you can read a script as it passes straight in front of a camera, or a piece of glass which is almost unseen between you and your audience. Instead of reading, or even glancing down at your notes on a table or lectern, you can look straight ahead and deliver your speech without hesitation.

At least, that's the way it is if you learn to use the system professionally! There are, however, a number of pitfalls.

Firstly, novices tend to become nervous (which shows!) because they think they're at the mercy of the system and its operator: what if they misread a word and need to correct it – or pause to cough – while the script relentlessly rolls on under the control of the operator?

Don't worry – it's not like that! The operator is skilled in varying the speed of the script to match the delivery of the speaker. If you stop, for whatever reason – hopefully the laughter and applause of your audience! – then the autoscript stops, too. If you slow down to emphasise a key point, or speed up your delivery for a throwaway aside, then the autoscript will change pace with you. Just like slides or any other aid, it is your servant and you will perform better if you have the knowledge and confidence to regard it as just that.

## MAKING THE MOST OF THE MEDIA

When required, by the way, autoscript systems can be supplied with hand or foot attachments so that the speed is directly controlled by the speaker.

But a cautionary note: like any piece of technology, however sophisticated, the autoscript can break down. You must be prepared for this. Firstly, you should be so familiar and at ease with your script that you could if necessary take up the theme at any point where the system breaks down, and ad lib your way from there. Secondly, you should have the 'second row defence' of a typed script on paper in front of you, so that you can use it as a prop in the event of breakdown. However, that is not as easy as it may sound: when the autoscript breaks down halfway into the speech, there's little point in having a script in front of you which still begins at page 1! So you need to familiarise yourself well beforehand with the paragraphs on autoscript which relate to a new page of typed words – and to turn the pages of type accordingly as you speak. That way, if the autoscript breaks down, you will look down at the typed version – and you'll be on the right page!

If you really want to become proficient at using this technique, observe the professionals. Watch leading politicians at party conferences, for example. They appear to look left, right and centre at their audiences as they address them from the rostrum. That's because they use not one, but three autoscript mirrors at different angles! You will notice how they occasionally look down at their notes even though every word is on autoscript in front of them. That's for two reasons – to signal a change of subject, and to try to con their audience into thinking that they have no autoscript in front of them and are speaking from the heart with no more than brief notes to guide them!

I don't propose to dwell on detail concerning all the new technology that is nowadays coming to the aid of the presenter: after all, this is not meant to be some technical manual. And the most sophisticated paraphernalia yet devised in the new multi-media environment cannot function in any worthwhile sense if the content, style and personal technique are not up to scratch.

Some more examples as illustration ...

I was 'anchoring' a major convention at Wembley (1000-seat

auditorium) for the high-earning representatives of one of Britain's biggest financial services and assurance groups. To give an idea of the calibre of people there, several were earning over £300 000 in personal commission. We had a number of the usual 'keynote addresses', some video reports on the big screen and some on-stage interviews which I conducted. Everything was leading up to the big motivational 'star presentation' to be given by one of America's most famous marketing gurus who had a reputation amounting almost to legendary proportions for his charismatic, inspirational skills as a speaker.

Let's call him Hank Jason to spare blushes all round. I talked to him very briefly before the 'show' (for that's what he would make it). That's to say, he talked to me – telling me exactly how he was to be introduced. I duly obliged.

'Ladies and gentlemen,' I said from my seat centre stage, 'this is supposed to be the moment we've all been waiting for – the moment when I welcome the great Hank Jason to our convention. Unfortunately, we have a problem. Hank has flown in from Los Angeles to join us – but there's been fog at Heathrow and his plane has been delayed. I understand it has now landed but ...'

At this point there was a shout from the very back of the tiered auditorium: 'Hold it, Mike. I've made it.' And he charged down the centre steps, bounded Superman-style on to the stage and raised his arms high as he turned to receive the rapturous applause of his audience. They were already half out of their seats and he'd hardly said a word.

I slipped into the wings and left this king of marketing hype to his adoring subjects. He had in a few seconds already taught me another lesson about the value of a strong start to a presentation. (Strong? Perhaps a better word would be nuclear.) And as I sat backstage listening to him, I learned much more. His pace was electrifying – and his pauses all so telling that you could almost touch the suspense in the air. He had them laughing until they cried with witty stories which were always pertinent and relevant to his theme. He tugged at all the emotions they possessed. He was brilliant and I felt duly humbled – a professional myself, I was realising my own inadequacies as a presenter.

Hank's 20 minutes were coming to a close and I stood in the

wings and straightened my tie, ready to walk on stage and express what would certainly be inadequate thanks for our star's roof-raising contribution to the convention ... Five minutes went by, then ten. The response from the audience began to diminish. Twenty minutes. Thirty. You could have heard a pin drop – for all the wrong reasons – among a silent audience. Eventually, well over an hour past his appointed time, Hank Jason ground to a halt.

That was something like ten years ago. And today, what might have been talked of as the ultimate example of presentation technique is still recalled by those who were there as possibly the greatest disaster ever to occur at the company's annual conventions.

We had all been taught a lesson, all right – the fundamental lesson that nobody is compelling enough to stretch audience interest and participation beyond its normal limits. Once again we come back to the rhetorical question which says it all: 'Have you ever listened to a speech that was too short?'

I remember, too, attending a seminar of an American-based association of professional communicators in business. It was held at BAFTA, that well-known Piccadilly home of excellence in communication – at least in the film and television arts.

Before the seminar began, we were given an information pack which included biographies of the speakers – and the full text of the president's keynote address. It seemed to me such a bright (and welcome) idea to provide this in writing for us. We would be able to read it and avoid the tedium of having to listen to the president delivering it. We could get on with the main presentations without having to sit through the usual platitudes. Another lesson for my personal list of experiences to learn from.

We assembled in our seats. The president entered stage left ... and proceeded to read the speech we had all just read for ourselves!

There are times, of course, when speeches need to be delivered in person even though they are available in print (with publication embargoes) beforehand: ministerial statements, which are to be published in the media, are obvious examples. But the BAFTA occasion was not one of those. It was, in fact, a very good example of how not to endear yourself to your audience!

I was once given the task of preparing half a dozen senior managers of a large high street retailing chain for their annual branch managers' conference. We arranged to meet in a studio at nine o'clock one morning for a rehearsal: I had told all of them to prepare their presentations so that we could rehearse them as many times as necessary (some would no doubt be 'naturals', others nervous wrecks who needed a lot of gentle nurturing).

They were, without exception, people on top of their jobs who held their own in a ruthlessly competitive business. They were well used to managing their staff and they certainly knew all there was to know about company policy, the products they sold, the marketing strategy and so on. Confident, 'laid-back', they arrived at the studio in various states of mind: one or two clearly felt the exercise was going to be a bit of fun – a break, at least, from the daily routine in the branch. Some had a rather supercilious air, regarding the rehearsal as a waste of time: all they had to do was talk to the employees about business they knew like the back of their hands.

By 9.30 that morning, I had sent them all away!

Not one of them understood that presentation is a skill which requires thorough training and never-ending practice. They had arrived with no preparation of any sort – no thought of the structure of their presentations, the messages they wanted to convey, the aids they might use to support their words, the nature of information they required to fulfil their brief, ideas to encourage participation from their audience ... in short, the way they might inform, entertain and motivate the company's branch managers.

Without doing their homework – and recognising that presentation techniques call for more skill than falling off a log – they would have been wasting the company's time and money going through the motions of a 'rehearsal'.

So I sent them home, rather like naughty schoolboys. A few days later we gathered together again. They had worked hard (some, I suspect, in front of the mirror at home) to prepare for what they now realised was a hard-won skill, and we developed together an in-house 'show' that in the event equipped branch managers (their audience) to do a better job selling the company's goods.

Presentational skills, you see, show up in the bottom line!

CHAPTER THIRTEEN

# The inside job ... lessons of the revolution

It was in the mid-1970s that the revolution happened. It changed my life – and it brought irrevocable change to the entire world of business.

Leaders of the revolution included Professor Alan Bullock and his colleagues who published in 1977 their report on industrial democracy. Shock, horror! The report dared to suggest that 'workers' should be told what was going on in the companies for whom they worked. This was, in the view of many people, a frightening concept – a clear confirmation that Britain was now careering down the slippery slope towards communism. Years of Labour administration and union-inspired industrial discontent had finally led to this.

At around the same time, another revolution was born. A technical breakthrough called 'video' was introduced. It would mean that the making of visual programmes was no longer to be only in the hands of Hollywood and the television giants (plus a relatively few enthusiasts with moving film facilities). It offered business particularly the means to communicate with employees and customers in a new and much more effective way than conventional methods allowed.

Bullock and video. In a sense, they were made for each other and the prospect excited me. I left mainstream television to set up a service for business, using the techniques of video to practise the principles of Bullock (which, after the initial alarm, were seen to be the unarguable way forward for progressive companies in commerce and industry).

My first clients were naturally the 'big boys' – companies who were able to afford what were in those early days quite high production costs, and who had a particular need to communicate with large numbers of employees around the globe. I remember, for example, that ICI had 190 000 employees in almost every corner of the world. Video was a wonderful new tool to enable management to show them all what was being achieved by all the divisions – and to explain company strategy. (Incidentally, there was one aspect of working conditions then that I believe will never return – company planes made available for shooting, first-class travel, best hotels and all expenses paid. They were the 'fat' days before the approaching age of redundancy and fierce cost-cutting.)

And with Taylor Woodrow we launched an in-house quarterly video magazine called *Team Television* which used an entertaining magazine format to inform and motivate team members. (Founder Frank Taylor would never countenance the use of words like 'employee' or 'director'. In that respect, he was wise before his time.)

Perhaps the most effective example of the power of this new medium in those early days came through a company called Allied Medical Group. This was a case history that displayed many facets of internal communication which are still valid today.

The company's chief role was to run major hospitals in Saudi Arabia and the United Arab Emirates. There was a continuous requirement to recruit nurses, specialists and paramedics to go and work in places like Riyadh and Abu Dhabi. At first, recruitment proved easy. Very high salaries with a tax-exemption arrangement between governments, plus the prospect of a working environment with the best equipment money could buy ... all this was most attractive to hard-pressed, ill-paid British nurses in particular.

But very soon, serious problems surfaced for AMG. Female nurses who went to Saudi Arabia were shocked on arrival to find conditions for which they had not been adequately prepared. No drinking, of course. No downtown shopping on their own. No casual clothes that didn't cover ankles and wrists. A living compound cut off from the outside community ... It was all difficult to cope with, and many nurses were tearing up their two-year contracts and returning home within a few weeks of starting work.

What was to be done to stop these defections which were costing the company a great deal of money – not to mention the damage to their reputation among their oil-rich government clients?

Clearly a communication exercise was called for – and video proved to be the tool that made it effective.

At the time, one of the most popular television programmes around was *The Good Life* sitcom. We embarked on a video programme called *The Good Life*? It set out to show exactly what life was like in Saudi and the UAE for medical staff going out there. It showed nurses enjoying the benefits – working with equipment that they could only dream of in the UK; swimming in the open-air pool in the Riyadh compound; talking of how they could earn enough in two years to buy a house with cash on their return home. But it also showed the downside. An AMG manager talked 'on camera' about the psychological pressures of work in that society – and particularly warned against people going out there to escape personal problems they may have had back home.

When we had made the first video, we showed the 'rough cut' to our client in London. 'Do you have to be quite so honest?' he asked.

I was emphatic about that. Yes, it was crucial to show the conditions, warts and all. To his credit, he agreed to the video as we had made it and issued an instruction that no would-be recruit could be allowed to sign a contract until he or she had seen the video.

The effect was dramatic. From the day that rule was applied, not one nurse failed to complete a contract. More astonishing was that recruitment actually increased. Nurses out there told me, on subsequent visits to update the video, that they had actually 'signed on' because of the honest approach of the programme. As one of them said to me: 'I thought, if the company is as honest as that, they must be worth working for.'

The first video cost AMG £25 000. It was calculated that they saved that much within a few days! And the lessons they (and we) learned were many. They remain valid today:

MAKING THE MOST OF THE MEDIA

1. It pays to tell the truth!
2. Honesty earns respect.
3. The cost of telling employees and prospective recruits the facts of working life is quickly recouped.
4. Video techniques are a potent way of delivering a message.

As a rule, of course, the job of internal communication in business needs to be tackled on a long-term basis. Deep-seated attitudes in a workforce can't be changed overnight.

Consider the case of Thames Water as it embarked on the traumatic change from public to private utility – and then sought to motivate its employees as partners in a customer-led enterprise (which would inevitably mean, among other things, substantial job losses).

'Managing change' has been a prime task for companies in the last three decades and for those in the throes of privatisation it was a particularly dramatic challenge to their skills of communication. For here was a burning political issue on top of everything else: making the most of the media opportunities was a task fraught with danger!

It was, of course, a challenge for external as well as internal communication techniques, but I'm concerned in this chapter only with the internal variety – the use of media like video and print to persuade the workforce to 'get behind' the privatised organisation.

The print was already in place. The utility's newspaper, *Thames Water News*, a monthly tabloid, was distributed to 13 000 employees and pensioners. It was a professional publication which informed readers of company matters in an entertaining fashion. Now it needed to change up several gears to effect nothing less than a revolution in everybody's attitudes and working practices.

Now that is not as simple as it might superficially appear, whatever the business. First and foremost, it calls for a tricky balancing act for top management.

The head of personnel (or human resources as the more fashionable job title has it) may recognise the need to be completely honest and even self-critical in the eyes of the workforce, but the financial director may find it especially painful

## THE INSIDE JOB ... LESSONS OF THE REVOLUTION

to authorise significant outlay on a journal that isn't an unadulterated propaganda sheet!

In the case of Thames Water, there was a refreshing (and ultimately rewarding) readiness to allow an outside agency to produce a newspaper which carried its fair share of unflattering news stories and critical correspondence. There was, of course, a huge information task to be fulfilled. A totally new culture was to replace the old; most working conditions and rewards were to be restructured in a climate of sometimes deep suspicion. (There was also the minefield created by statutory financial regulations, which meant that all 'copy' for the newspaper which contained any elements possibly affecting the ultimate Stock Exchange flotation had to be submitted for independent clearance.)

The medium chosen to tackle the most sensitive issues was video.

One of the commonest mistakes made by companies embarking on an internal communications exercise is the 'talking down' approach. Classically, the chairman or chief executive delivers a 'sermon'. It's obviously on Autocue. It may well be badly delivered. (Who has the guts in an organisation to tell the chairman he's not a very bright communicator and needs lessons?) And it is probably a 'committee script', drafted and redrafted by a number of jargon-ridden sycophants in head office who will be particularly happy if the message sounds weighty but actually says nothing of significance. Above all, it is a one-way process that leaves no room for that key element, *listening*, and is therefore received by the audience with cynical disregard.

The first video exercise in Thames Water was planned to reflect the workforce's concerns and inevitable ignorance about the effects of privatisation. Would it mean wholesale redundancies? What would happen to nationalised industry pensions? Would union strength be eroded? And so on.

To put such questions effectively to top management was not, however, a simple matter. The obvious technique – of asking manual workers, technicians and office staff to be recorded putting their questions to the chairman – was not really satisfactory because few were willing to do so. They were either too shy, or anxious that any critical question might cost them their job, or so suspicious of the exercise that they thought they were being tricked into playing management's game. Words like 'trust' and 'credibility' were in short supply during those days of confrontation!

The solution was to send an independent, apolitical television current affairs presenter (me, as a matter of fact!) round company offices and depots, persuading employees to air their anxieties. I then put the hard questions on camera to the chairman and managing director, asking supplementary questions of my own if I felt their initial answers were obscure or incomplete.

Using the medium of video in this way was only a beginning. Distributed to every department in the company, it notched up only a lukewarm reception. As a 'one-off' exercise it would have been quickly forgotten. But in the years that have followed privatisation, Thames Water have invested substantial resources in the production of a quarterly video programme which has become bolder in its approach as its credibility has been gradually built up. Nowadays, there are programmes devoted to such delicate issues as job security and the need to change. The videos have become much more than instruments of information and education: they are now really sounding-boards to enable managers to *listen* to the ideas of their better-empowered teams. There's a formal system of 'reporting back' so that the workforce's views and suggestions are recorded, to enable a response in turn from management. Put another way, communication is not a top-down process but a truly circular one. The effect on morale and motivation has been exciting.

The advent of multimedia and a whole raft of new techniques have given businesspeople a new set of opportunities for communicating with their 'troops', though it must be said that huge sums of money can be poured down the drain if they're misused. There are great benefits, for example, in some of the new interactive techniques. Clearly, indeed by definition, they allow for a two-way spread of information and ideas. But there's little point in spending, say, £100 000 to produce a sophisticated CD-Rom if only a tiny proportion of the workforce have the means to play it! There really are circumstances whereby a typed announcement on noticeboards in offices and shopfloors is, to this day, the most effective way of getting a message across!

## THE INSIDE JOB ... LESSONS OF THE REVOLUTION

Whatever the medium, these are my basic rules for internal communication in business:

1. *Listen.* (Yes, I'll keep coming back to that little word until the very last page of this book!) Given half a chance, your audience may have more valuable ideas to contribute to the company's welfare than you imagine.

2. *Don't lecture* your audience. There's nothing better guaranteed to alienate them than a 'sermon' from the boss laying down the law. If you play the autocrat or take on the mantle of executive infallibility, the best response you're likely to earn is a cynical sneer.

3. *Respect* those watching or listening or reading your words – and show that respect by inviting their participation in managing the company's progress (currently the buzz word is 'empowerment').

4. *Respond* to their participation by being seen to act on the feedback you receive.

5. *Invest long-term* in the most effective means of communication. A single video or in-house newsletter can't do the job of moving minds. Earning trust and credibility takes time.

6. *Use the best media.* Your message may be faultless but it won't strike home if you use the wrong medium. An e-mail announcement won't do the job if half your employees work in the field, far from any computer terminal. In that case, try the Royal Mail instead – to their homes!

7. *Measure the impact.* Don't rely on 'gossip' to determine how effective your message is. The manager who assures you that your annual review was 'very well received, sir' may give you a completely false impression. Invest in serious 'audience research' to give yourself the real picture.

8. *Know thyself!* That was the exhortation of the Oracle and it may be the most difficult of all personal rules to follow in business. The fact that you may be the best chief executive a company could have doesn't mean you're the best communicator. If you

use visual media particularly – like video – record your 'performance' and play it over again and again, honestly searching for strengths and weaknesses to enable you to do better next time. Call in a professional outsider who can be trusted to give you an unbiased assessment rather than the sycophantic appraisal of an employee, however senior.

9. *Come clean.* In a later chapter I offer a checklist for facing the external media. It includes the exhortation to 'tell the truth'. This is equally important when you are communicating internally. The only difference is that there may be financial restrictions and regulations that prevent certain information being divulged ahead of its release to the City and the Stock Exchange. But please don't use that as an excuse for denying other important information to employees. Withholding or distorting the facts will have the ultimate effect of nullifying all the trust you have rightly worked hard (and spent significantly) to build in your business.

CHAPTER FOURTEEN
· · · · · · · · · · · · · · · ·

# Do-it-yourself media promotion ... how to score now the goalposts have been moved

Even if you seek professional assistance to promote your business through the media (and surprise, surprise, I strongly advise you to do so!) it's as well for you to understand the most effective ways to do so – and the rules of the game.

So let's consider now the opportunities of getting your message across by what PR people like to call 'proactive' means. (In other words, you originate ideas that may hit the airwaves or the headlines without 'waiting for something to happen' to which you can react.)

In television, an increasingly popular vehicle is the VNR – video news release. Essentially it's the same as a written press release, except that it's produced on video. It also costs a great deal more! And it demands attention to a great range of factors which may influence the broadcasters to use it. (Remember, you pay for the production, distribution and monitoring of a VNR. The broadcasting organisations get it free. That may sound enormously attractive to them, but they are properly very pernickety about using unsolicited promotional material submitted in the guise of 'news' and, as we shall see, there are fairly tough guidelines in both public service and commercial television about the use of such material.)

Producing a VNR – anything from two to four minutes long –

calls for the same techniques as any other company video made for training, marketing and similar purposes. But it's essential that it has genuine news value and that it's designed for the right audience or programmes you want to persuade to transmit it.

Distribution through the right channels is the key to success. A monitoring system is also important: finding out exactly where and when your VNR is used around the world will not only enable you to check its cost-effectiveness but will also provide valuable lessons to be learned for the next time you use this type of promotion.

In my experience, Reuters Television are the leaders in this field and it's instructive to quote excerpts from their message to a company who wanted to produce a VNR pegged to a visit to their headquarters by the Queen when they won an award for exporting. (The company had already been given strict guidelines on the restrictions on use of footage featuring Her Majesty, especially the prohibition on using her as a commercial promotion for the company and its products.)

Reuters wrote:

> News value: We believe your story will prove sufficiently attractive to be picked up by broadcasters. In the UK the Queen's presence will add weight to the story; the challenge will come outside the UK where the Queen's presence may be less attractive.
>
> Much depends on the quality of the footage. We will ask you to supply a short voiced version (called an 'A' roll) as well as a selection of rushes with natural sound ('B' role).

Outlets to be targeted – and those where there seemed little chance of exciting the broadcasters' interest – were then detailed. The message continued:

> We normally advise against distributing VNRs on a Friday (the day of the Queen's visit) but in this case we do not believe that it will be a disadvantage.
>
> Your story will only be perceived as 'hard' news in the UK. Other outlets are likely to see the story as good feature material although some may want to use it same-day. The weekend is the ideal time to distribute a financial feature story

because Monday morning's financial news programmes, particularly on breakfast news shows, have little to report before the week's business begins. This will probably give us our best opportunity for exposure ... It is likely that some outlets, particularly in the UK, will want to run a preview story on the morning of the visit. You may lose opportunities for exposure if this is not available.

That's just a taste of the very detailed homework that needs to be done before you embark on a VNR. 'Selling-in' to broadcasters needs to be undertaken a week or so before the day of issuing the tapes. Satellite transmission time needs to be arranged for overseas as well as the usual channels for UK distribution. And so much more. Getting your few minutes, or even seconds, of exposure on domestic and global TV screens needs significant input of time, professional and technical skills, and money – but we have already seen how great are the rewards.

Ask about costs and you'll get the usual answer about the length of a piece of string! But Reuters says 'As a guide, an average cost of production, distribution and monitoring in a single European country is between £8000 and £12 000. A Europe-wide service concentrating on national broadcasters costs £12 000 to £25 000.'

Purely sound tapes for distribution to radio stations – sometimes called ANRs, or audio news releases – are naturally in a different league as far as cost is concerned. But don't be fooled into thinking they're easy to make. If anything, they are more difficult to 'sell' to the broadcasters than VNR. Certainly the BBC has become rather snooty about accepting tapes for its local radio stations.

Nevertheless, there are more than 160 local independent radio stations, and many of them are strapped for cash, so an acceptable ANR may be given air time – sometimes, indeed, several airings at different times of day.

What do they regard as 'acceptable'? Well, the tape should have a news peg – that's to say, it should reflect in some way a straight news story of the day. It should not overtly, or too brashly, sing the praises of a commercial interest. It should be genuinely interesting and produced at least to the standards of the radio station transmitting it.

For example, let's assume that a government press release has announced an upsurge in statistics of new house building. You are an estate agency called Bloggs and Co. On the day of the release, you offer your local radio station a taped interview – possibly with a 'name' interviewer who is well respected in current affairs radio or TV programmes. It goes something like this:

*Interviewer*: As you've heard on the news, more new houses are being built in Britain after a period of decline. What effect will this have on the housing market, on prices and availability? Joe Smith, as managing director of local agent Bloggs and Co., how do you see the market developing?

Joe Smith provides answers which are (here we go again!) educative, informative and entertaining. Only once in the course of a three-minute interview does he mention his firm's name again ('Obviously I can't answer for others in this locality but we at Bloggs and Co. are experiencing ...'). He doesn't attempt any 'hard sell' and certainly makes no claims about his agency being the best in the business locally. What he does achieve is an image of authority – the man the media would turn to for reliable information – and the name of his agency, though mentioned only twice, will stay in the minds of those listeners who may be thinking of buying or selling a house.

From the radio station's point of view, the story is topical; it has been given a local angle; it features a well-known interviewer thus adding some prestige to the station's output; and it contains genuine information. To cover that angle of the story, the station would have had to set up a very similar item anyway – probably with the same Joe Smith – so there are solid reasons for accepting the tape at no cost to themselves.

There are other ways of promoting your company or your product – like sponsorship of programmes or (a growing activity, this) so-called 'product placement'. Although it may be argued that the broadcasting rules to do with 'free' commercial promotion are now tighter than they were, it's also true that they're different. The goalposts have been moved so that, to give a single example – sponsorship – is now permitted albeit within strict boundaries in a way it once was not.

According to the ITC (Independent Television Commission, the commercial sector's watchdog) 'product placement is not frowned upon – it is prohibited'. That sounds clear enough, yet the fact is that product placement in all the media has become a thriving business!

My purpose here is certainly not to help businesspeople bend the rules in these matters – but to promote themselves within the letter and even the spirit of the programme codes and regulations. For instance, the ITC has advised producers of programmes for television to avoid what it calls 'puffery' and in furthering that cause, Meridian Broadcasting has issued its own guidance to producers: 'Avoid flowery language ... beware adjectives that can tip the balance away from editorial justification into a plug for a brand or service ... Make sure presenters and interviewees don't eulogise – when in doubt, cut the adjectives out.'

It's clear – and in my view absolutely right – that the broadcasters are determined to prevent the improper commercial exploitation of their editorial output. But that does not prevent your making the most of the media! In my example above of Joe Smith the estate agent, I used no flowery adjectives. Bloggs and Co. was not even referred to as the locality's 'leading' agency, though it might have been. Yet both Joe Smith and the agency would benefit greatly simply by being there and by earning the respect of listeners in the various ways discussed in earlier chapters.

I'm constantly surprised by business executives who not only fail to take the sort of proactive steps outlined here to utilise the media, but also miss opportunities to *react*.

In my early radio broadcasting days on the BBC's World Service, I presented a programme called *New Ideas*. It was intended to feature inventions, new designs and products as a kind of shop window for overseas listeners. It blatantly promoted British exports, even to the extent of giving names and addresses of suppliers. All at no cost to the companies concerned.

My task was to call up the manufacturers or distributors to find out more about their products and invite them to be interviewed. No catch. No controversy. Just plain promotion! Yet time and again I was met by suspicion or, at best, failure to seize the opportunity. 'Mr Brown is in a meeting ... on holiday ... not available today ...' I found it hard to believe that executives hoping to make a profit could turn down completely free and powerful global advertising through laziness or – more likely – a total lack of appreciation of the beneficial power of the media.

They badly needed training. Which brings me to my next chapter.

## CHAPTER FIFTEEN

# The benefits of training ... and how to go shopping for the best package

Whenever I interview people for a job in my production company, I invariably ask applicants 'What do you think is your greatest personal strength?'

And the answer, also invariably? 'Well, I'm very good with people ...' It's extraordinary how many of us are deluded about our own charms and magnetic personalities! By the same token, business executives tend to believe that they are 'natural' communicators with instinctive persuasive powers. For many of them, of course, this misplaced self-belief stems from years of working with sycophantic underlings giving them the impression that they can do no wrong.

Whatever the reasons, the fact is (as years of working in this field have taught me) that most executives are in great need of training to face the media – and often it's the ones right at the top of the management pile who are most in need.

Professionals spend their lives perfecting their presenting and interviewing and public speaking skills to a point where everything looks easy. Indeed, that is one of their main aims – because that's the way to put an audience at its ease, too. The danger is that businesspeople in particular fail to understand the years of hard work and practice that are needed.

However, I must assume that the readers of this book are aware of the need to be trained, so now we turn to the tricky question of where to look for the best training companies. In some ways, this is rather like choosing a doctor: as a lay person with no knowledge of medical matters, you have no yardsticks for assessing the skills of medics in your locality – perhaps until it's too late! So I suggest that the first thing to do is 'ask around': talk to people from other companies who've been through the training process to find out which trainers are best recommended (just as you'd ask the neighbours about doctors or solicitors when moving into a new locality).

Then ask two or three recommended trainers to suggest what they might do for you – and, of course, what it will cost! The best, I believe, will tell you something like this ...

The session(s) should be tailor-made to your own particular needs. So the trainer must first be given a thorough background to you personally and your company's mission. There must be complete trust and confidentiality between both parties. After all, part of the objective is to equip you to cope with any kind of question or approach from the media – and that won't be possible if you fail to disclose to the trainer any skeletons in your cupboard which might be discovered by painstaking media researchers. Similarly, you will need to reveal industrial or commercial secrets, like the prospective launch of a new product that's still under wraps. The need for this trust is another good reason for checking out the trainer with other companies, to be sure that confidences will be well placed.

The training should take place well away from your office or factory. It's going to be important to give you as 'real' a taste of media grilling as possible and the cosy, familiar surroundings of your own place will not provide that. You should also ensure that you cannot be distracted by company matters, so breaks in training 'to call the office' or persistently ringing mobile phones should be banned. Training at this level will only be effective if you regard it as the highest priority – and demonstrate that fact to those around you. So your assistants must know that you are no more to be disturbed or distracted than you would be in the middle of a monthly board meeting.

The location should reflect as far as possible the atmosphere of

## THE BENEFITS OF TRAINING ...

television and radio studios. (Training will also encompass the press, but most of the emphasis is likely to be on the broadcast media.) It is useful if an actual transmission studio is used, but cost and other factors may preclude this and the desired environment can be achieved by setting up cameras, lights, microphones and all the other technical paraphernalia in almost any secure location.

Avoid joining 'mixed' groups. That's to say, arrange training exclusively for your own company personnel rather than 'off-the-shelf' sessions with people from elsewhere which will obviously prevent the airing of sensitive confidential issues. It will also result in hands-on exercises which are lacking in necessary impact because they are unrealistic. All the trainer can do in these circumstances is to play games – sometimes called role-playing. You may be told, for example, to imagine that your factory has been burned to the ground and then asked 'tough' questions about the 'disaster'. You may regard that as an amusing and even stimulating way to practise interview techniques, but I can assure you it doesn't compare with exercises that spring surprise near-the-bone questions at you about issues which are of very real current concern!

It's essential, in my view, to be trained in groups of four or five colleagues. If you're the company chairman and acutely conscious of your weaknesses in confrontational situations, it will be difficult for you to expose those weaknesses in front of people under your management control. But you will get far more value out of the training by doing just that: the challenge (fed by large doses of your adrenalin!) of performing in front of them is a crucial part of the training process.

It is, of course, relatively cheaper to arrange training in groups. The costs of trainers, operators, equipment and so on are virtually the same whether one person is on the course or five.

Another good reason for the group approach is that it enables a company to choose its best spokesperson in the light of this experience. Although almost anybody can be trained to improve performance, it's an obvious fact that some will prove to be better than others – and who the 'stars' are can only be discovered after pursuing the training routine. Frequently, in my experience, the best performers are at first sight the most unlikely ones! The

## MAKING THE MOST OF THE MEDIA

energetic chief executive, the suave marketing manager, the attractive human resources director ... they may all crumble in front of the cameras while the quiet, seemingly uncharismatic financial controller blossoms as the real image-builder your company needs. (Incidentally, most of the major stars of my acquaintance – the ones who are in their element captivating large audiences – are shy, introverted people. That apparent paradox is the subject of another book altogether.)

All senior people in your company should have training in communication skills, but it's also a worthwhile idea to select one or two as preferred spokespeople who may receive extra, more sophisticated, training. And in selecting those people, the value of a reputable, established training company is that it will recommend the right people without regard to company politics (or kowtowing to the chief executive who signs the cheques!). The trainer will supply an appraisal of all pupils after a session. If you are the boss, be prepared for a sobering critique of your performance and be 'big' enough to assign the role of company spokesperson to someone else if that is the professional recommendation.

There may be, of course, circumstances in which the one-to-one approach is unavoidable. I was approached, for example, to help a managing director who was acknowledged in his sector of the industry to be brilliant – but who had a serious problem in communicating with his own staff. He wanted to, and realised the importance of doing so, but there was still an invisible barrier between him and them. I met him for a letting-the-hair-down lunch to try to understand the nature of his difficulty before suggesting a training approach. 'One of my biggest handicaps,' he told me, 'is that I can't remember names – and I know that in a small company like ours, I need to develop good personal relationships.'

I muttered something about his being a fairly common failing when he interrupted:

'I doubt if you can understand quite how bad it is. Last night, for example, I attended a rather high-powered cocktail party with my wife. One of the guests was a major client of ours – but as I went to introduce him to my wife, suddenly I forgot her name – and we've been married for 20 years.'

As I said, there *are* special needs which call for individual, personal help – but as a rule, the small group is the best approach.

My own, perhaps unconventional, belief is that media training should not last longer than half a day in the first instance. That's because the work is so intense that pupils are – or should be – extremely tired after a four-hour session. And there is so much to absorb, as we shall see when we put some training experiences on the printed page in the next chapter.

The usual pattern of a training session will be something like this:

1. *Introductory talk.* Your trainer – someone who is well known as a media insider, though not necessarily a presenter – talks about the right attitude to media exposure and the way to profit from it.

2. *First exercise.* To familiarise those who have no experience with the techniques of studio work, each trainee is interviewed 'on camera' for three or four minutes on a factual, non-controversial topic.

3. *Playback and analysis.* The interviews are played back and analysed in group session. Strengths and weaknesses begin to become apparent, so the training starts to become more focused on individual needs.

4. *Second exercise.* This time, much more aggressive and controversial interviews are recorded – on issues which particularly affect the interviewees' own company.

5. *More analysis.* The playbacks are now analysed in a more demanding way and the lessons to be drawn become more sophisticated.

From here onwards, the nature of the session varies according to the weaknesses that have become apparent in the exercises. There may be more 'hands-on' exercises, or lecturing, or question-and-answer sessions.

Before each exercise, the trainer will give the group notice of the topic to be pursued in interview and the area of questioning. Time – say, 15 minutes – will be provided for the group to discuss among themselves the questions likely to be asked; the best answers from the company point of view; and the way to make opportunities for company promotion. In a sense, these breaks for preparation are the best guide to a group's appreciation of the value of the training. As in real circumstances, working hard on 'preparing for battle' is the most important factor of all – and trainees who use the period for a relaxed gossip will quickly get their comeuppance in the interview exercise.

At the end of a session, trainees may be given a check-list. I think this is a useful aid for keeping in your office desk drawer for reference whenever the call comes to be interviewed. Rather like a pilot before take-off, you can run through each point in the list to refresh your mind about key lessons you've been taught. Here's an example:

Tell the *truth*.

Keep your *eyes steady* and look at the interviewer.

*Listen* to what's being asked to make sure you *answer the question*.

Take every reasonable opportunity to promote your company. (On television, the time you're given is worth £200 000 a minute!)

Remember that television has six times the impact of printed words, so *use it* and *welcome it*.

*Don't drink* alcohol beforehand.

*Relax* (shoulders down, breathe deeply, do mouth exercises) but at the same time, *never for a second lose concentration*.

Take every opportunity to show that you really *care* – about your company, your staff, your customers, etc.

Do your *homework* so that you're as well informed as possible. (Remember that your superior knowledge gives you a huge advantage over your interviewer.)

In discussion, *don't lose your temper*.

## THE BENEFITS OF TRAINING...

Use *language* to best effect – try to use short simple words and always eschew the jargon of your business.

*Smile* – in the right places.

Avoid monotony – *vary* the pattern of your sentences and the speed of delivery.

Be seen to be *proud* of what you and your company do.

There's one other service you should expect from a training company – a kind of permanent 'helpline'. This means that when a request does come to face the media, you can call up your trainer and ask for specific advice over the telephone about the line likely to be taken by the programme or interviewer concerned. Most programmes have styles of their own and a trainer who's also an 'insider' will be well equipped to tell you – or warn you! – about them. For example, one well-known investigative interviewer has a technique of asking a question and then, after an answer has been provided, saying nothing but nodding and looking at you straight in the eye. If you're not prepared for this, you may think that more needs to be said and start to panic. That's when you could blurt out something you didn't mean to say. If you have been warned of the interviewer's technique beforehand, you'll have the confidence to keep mum and stare him out.

One final word about the training process. It is not the good trainer's objective to turn out clones! In other words, the last thing he or she wants is to make you look and perform to a pattern. There are basic rules, which I've outlined in previous pages, but they are not meant to suppress your own personality. A bland, colourless performer may follow every rule in the book and still fail to make the most of the media.

Remember: educate, inform and *entertain*!

# CHAPTER SIXTEEN

## Practice session ... the 'easy' interview that can be difficult

Let's now translate to the printed page an exercise which could be staged in the sort of practice session outlined in the previous chapter.

What follows is easy – or it should be!

You're the chief executive of a computer services company called COMP. You have been asked to appear in a television programme called *Careerline,* to be interviewed on the subject of career opportunities for young people in the IT industry. You've been told that the programme is part of a series which attempts to help young people choose and pursue careers. It is transmitted in the late evening. Its audience profile indicates viewers aged between 16 and 25, and their parents. Your interview will last approximately three minutes.

See first how it can go wrong ...

*Interviewer*: Mr Brown, what advice would you give a 16-year-old school leaver thinking of a career in the IT industry?

*Chief executive*: Well, I'd tell him that information technology is a very exciting industry to be in. There's such a wide variety of jobs available. It's a modern industry which is still growing so there are plenty of opportunities for a young man who's eager to work and is ambitious.

*Interviewer*: Yes, but what should our school leaver do? For instance, is it a good idea to leave at 16 or do most companies require higher qualifications nowadays?

*Chief executive*: Oh, it's up to him, really. I mean, there are plenty of jobs for youngsters of his age if he's prepared to start at the bottom ...

*Interviewer*: Like unqualified office boy, you mean?

*Chief executive*: Well, yes. I mean, we've all got to start somewhere. I'm trying to explain that in these days of high unemployment, a lad should be grateful for all the opportunities ...

*Interviewer*: But Mr Brown, we're talking of young people who want to carve a *career* in IT. Let me put my question another way: what sort of qualifications are desirable to make a good start in the industry?

*Chief executive*: Well, the better your qualifications, the better your chances.

*Interviewer*: Specialised qualifications or simply a good degree, perhaps?

*Chief executive*: Ah, well, this lad we were talking about ...

*Interviewer*: Excuse me, Mr Brown, but I didn't have a 'lad' as you call him in mind. A 16-year-old might be a girl. Are there equal opportunities for girls in the industry?

*Chief executive*: Oh, yes. Plenty.

*Interviewer*: How many women hold senior positions in your own company for instance?

*Chief executive*: Well, not senior positions exactly but there are several girls in the general office nowadays.

*Interviewer*: That rather sounds as though it is a male-dominated industry. What are the rewards?

*Chief executive*: Well, they're very good really. I mean, programmers and people like that can earn a good living – better than working in retail, let's say.

## PRACTICE SESSION...

*Interviewer*: Can you put a figure on it – the kind of salary a 23-year-old might earn, for example, entering the industry with a good degree in computer technology?

*Chief executive*: That's difficult – I mean, it would depend on how much specialised training might be needed in-house. But I'm in the marketing department and I'm not sure what the exact rates are in the technical side.

*Interviewer*: Where can young people find out more about the industry and how to enter it?

*Chief executive*: Oh, well, I should think the best idea would be to write to a computer firm in the locality where they live. Most companies have training or personnel officers who could give them more details.

*Interviewer*: Thank you, Mr Brown, I'm afraid that's all we have time for. It does seem that the computer industry is no place for ambitious girls and there's no clear entry pattern, but let's turn to our next career subject ...

Now you may think the scenario above is an exaggerated one, devised to illustrate as many gaffes as possible for the purposes of this book. But I assure you it's quite typical of a hundred such exercises I have witnessed in training sessions. It's all so simple – and yet seemingly so difficult for first-timers to grasp.

For a start, you could watch that interview and at the end of it still be asking what company the chief executive represented! It would have been so easy to say at least once something like: 'I can't answer for every company in the industry, of course, but at COMP ...' and go on to make a positive point that would have amounted to a priceless recruitment advertisement, yet well within the watchdog guidelines.

The overall impression was that the chief executive had completely wasted everybody's time, which would have left viewers with an extremely negative impression of his company. What would parents and their youngsters, hungry for information, have felt about waiting up late in the evening to watch an interview which gave them no useful information whatsoever? They'd surely be angry – and resolved not to turn to COMP when seeking a job.

There were so many more mistakes. The assumption in the very first answer that a 16-year-old job seeker would be a boy, for instance. That showed lack of concentration from a chief executive who wasn't thinking fast enough about his audience. I'm not asking for 'political correctness' – just for plain common sense!

The interview was spattered with 'wells' and 'I means'. That's laziness again, an indication that the interviewee is simply not working hard enough.

What kind of practical help is it for a young career-seeker to be told that there are 'exciting' opportunities without being given a single factual clue as to what they may be?

There was the patronising bit: 'A lad should be grateful for all the opportunities.' Angering the viewers again!

There was the fundamental failure to listen to the questions so that an exasperated interviewer had to resort to 'Let me put my question another way.'

Then there was the classic example of thoughtless, empty boasting about 'plenty of equal opportunities', which led the chief executive's own firm to be exposed as a very backward example of sex equality.

The question about rewards proved a disaster on more than one level. Surely the chief executive should have first made the point that 'rewards' are not exclusively financial. There are other important ones that attract young people – a good working environment; the satisfaction of quality workmanship; fast-track promotion for the ambitious; exciting developments in the technology of the future, and so many more. He could have warmed to his subject with telling examples of these kinds of reward culled from his own company's operations. Then, in turning to salary levels, he should have done his homework and arrived in the studio with factual examples like £20 000 for a graduate trainee programmer or something of the sort.

As it was, the whole interview desperately lacked the kind of basic information that job seekers need – addresses and phone numbers of organisations able to help them, for instance. He didn't even have the wit to suggest viewers write to him at COMP for more guidance!

## PRACTICE SESSION ...

The last comment of the interviewer illustrated a common peril – that of a 'summing-up' critical comment right at the end of an interview, leaving a bad taste (and sometimes a false one) in the mind of the viewer. Normally I would counsel interviewees to be alert to this danger and interrupt to prevent this damaging kind of summation. Unhappily, in the example we've recorded, the chief executive had no cause to complain, because the impression he had given thoroughly warranted the caustic conclusion!

The difference between that interview and the one that might have been could be estimated in cash terms to the tune of hundreds of thousands of pounds. Just consider the might-have-been version (and note how the questions become different as the inevitable consequence of more skilful answers):

*Interviewer*: Mr Brown, what advice would you give a 16-year-old school leaver thinking of a career in the IT industry?

*Chief executive*: Probably not to leave school at 16! It is possible for a boy or girl to enter the industry at the bottom with few academic qualifications – but in these days of fierce competition with honours graduates flocking into the industry, a youngster would have self-imposed mountains to climb by starting as some kind of office junior.

*Interviewer*: So are you advising university and a specialised degree as the best way in?

*Chief executive*: Not necessarily specialised. There are many firms which believe that the most important factor is evidence of a young person's 'brainpower'. In other words, they'll look for really good degrees in almost any subject on the basis that a good, well-disciplined mind can more easily be trained to absorb the company's own technical methods. My own company, COMP, for example, spends a million pounds a year training graduate recruits – even if they come to us with IT-related degrees! On the other hand, there are companies who insist on honours degrees in some aspect of computer technology.

*Interviewer*: You make it sound a tough career to break into.

*Chief executive*: For most young people who are ambitious to get to the very top in the industry it certainly is – but there are many attractions for young people at the same time. It's an astonishingly fast-growing industry so in the most progressive firms there are always vacancies. (We're looking for 80 people right now!) There are plenty of examples of enterprising, ambitious youngsters – some without university backgrounds – who have shown it to be an industry of opportunity by becoming millionaires in their thirties and forties!

*Interviewer*: So where should young people watching us now turn for more help and information?

*Chief executive*: They should ask their careers teachers at school or college, of course – and possibly visit their local careers centre (most towns have one). I suggest they might pick up some of the industry journals like *Computer Weekly* to get a feel for what's going on in the industry and to see the kind of jobs that are being advertised, with the qualifications being sought. Approach local companies for advice. I'll be happy to help, too. Would you like me to give my address?

*Interviewer*: That would be very helpful. We'll put it on screen at the end of this interview ... the last question, though: you've mentioned the millionaires, but for most average achievers, what are the rewards?

*Chief executive*: First and foremost, I think, is job satisfaction. It's an enormously exciting industry, developing at a furious pace and opening up opportunities literally to change the ways everybody works and lives. As for money, salaries are a good deal higher than in most jobs at an early age. 'Starters' straight from university for example, could easily earn £20 000 a year, with rapid increases.

*Interviewer*: I think I'll change jobs! Mr Brown, thank you. Now, your address for viewers who'd like more information ...

So there you have an interview which began with exactly the same question as the previous disaster. Yet it will be worth a great deal of money to Mr. Brown's company – not just as a free recruitment exercise, but by promoting the COMP image with long-lasting effect. And it didn't break the rules of 'puffery'.

## PRACTICE SESSION ...

Offering help was a perfectly acceptable ploy in the context of the programme.

Note how the interviewer's questions become much kinder – simply because Mr Brown's answers are positive and informative with no dubious comments which require nailing. There are also fewer questions, which is the way it should be. After all, the viewers haven't switched on to hear a list of clever questions: it's answers they're after! Often when I discuss an interview before going on air, I say to my subject: 'This will be ideal if I ask the first question and then you fill the rest of the time.' However, I then add a realistic rider: 'That probably won't happen because you may lose the thread or forget to mention salient points, so that I will need to prompt you – but let's at least make it our aim because it's you, not me, that the viewers want to see and hear.'

The danger inherent in all I've written in this chapter is that performing well (and profitably) seems deceptively simple. The skills *are* basic, but they need to be learned nevertheless! They require not only professional training but also painstaking preparation to arrive at the ultimate goal of making it all look easy.

Strangely enough, the tough, controversial interview may seem much more difficult but may actually be easier – simply because the questions often demand more straightforward answers. Anyway, we shall see ...

## CHAPTER SEVENTEEN

## More practice ... the 'difficult' interview that can be easy!

Time now to return to the scenario we began to envisage in Chapter 6 – the *TV Newswide* item about a pain-killing drug which has been on the market and prescribed by doctors for some time. It is now being put about in the press that the drug may eventually produce harmful side-effects.

This has all the elements of a tricky interview for the pharmaceutical company which manufactures and markets the drug. Millions of pounds are at stake – that's the commercial measure of the controversy. Millions of lives may be at risk – that's the human calculation.

Globomin was hailed, when it was introduced into Britain three years previously, as a major leap forward in the alleviation of arthritis. Doctors began to prescribe it with confidence to their patients and the manufacturers, Farmer Pharmaceuticals, built up an impressive dossier of case histories and patients' testimonials to back up a multi-million-pound promotional campaign within the medical profession – trade press advertising, a monthly video report to every GP's surgery, lavish (though discreet) entertaining – the lot. In charge of Farmers' marketing is Ron Stuch, who has been booked to be interviewed by Bill of *TV Newswide*.

The confrontation could go something like this ...

*Bill* (to camera): Today there have been more disturbing reports of arthritis sufferers taking the drug Globomin who have suffered

## MAKING THE MOST OF THE MEDIA

harmful and painful side-effects. There has even been one reported case of a death, though it is too early to confirm that this has been directly caused by the drug. Globomin is manufactured and distributed in this country by Farmer Pharmaceuticals whose marketing director is Ron Stuch. Mr Stuch, why have you not withdrawn your drug from the market?

*Ron*: Well, Bill, as they say, you shouldn't believe everything you read in the newspapers! We have been selling Globomin for three years now and thousands of people can tell you how much it has relieved the pain of arthritis.

*Bill*: But that's not the point of my question. As I said, there is growing evidence of harmful side-effects and even a fatality. Don't you think the drug should be withdrawn until more research is carried out?

*Ron*: Evidence? What evidence? The drug was thoroughly tested over many years and Farmers invested millions of pounds in its research and development before it was licensed for prescription. You can't expect us to waste all that investment just because of some unsubstantiated tittle-tattle in the popular papers.

*Bill*: But the public will expect you to show more concern about fears which have been reflected not only in the papers but also in the professional journals. Have you not considered at least investigating the reported cases and withholding supplies until Globomin is proved to be safe?

*Ron*: We have no doubts about the efficiency and safety of the drug. Many doctors have told us what a boon it has been to patients whom they regarded as untreatable before ...

*Bill*: Yes, I see that's a claim you make in some of the literature and tapes and disks you have been issuing to GPs in the last year or two. Indeed, your campaign to market Globomin to the profession has been high-powered – and expensive. How much have you spent on promoting the drug in the last three years?

*Ron*: Oh, I couldn't say ...

*Bill*: But you're the marketing director. You must know!

*Ron*: Well, we can't really quantify ...

*Bill* (interrupting): A million pounds? Two million?

*Ron*: I'm not sure that I can ...

*Bill*: Mr Stuch, we have seen some of your promotional campaign material and heard about the lavish entertaining, golf days and all the rest which you have used to persuade GPs. Are you not prepared to spend even a fraction of that money to pay for more research into safety – or do we have to wait for another human disaster of thalidomide proportions?

And so it may go on. There are those who will say that the interview was 'aggressive'. Ron Stuch will complain that he wasn't given a fair chance to state his case. Farmer Pharmaceuticals will complain loudly about 'trial by television'.

But Ron deserved everything he got. His answers were careless – and uncaring. His opening, dismissive response to press criticism gave the impression that the health and safety of patients – thousands of whom would be listening – was not of real concern to him. No wonder the interviewer became more pressing!

He seemed to put profit and loss before people, implying that the money his company had spent on research and development was somehow a more important factor than the subsequent protection of patients.

His reluctance to disclose promotional spending (and the dubious morality of entertainment expenses) was a good example of interviewees who fail to do their homework. It's obvious that in an issue like this, there are likely to be questions about advertising spend, so he should have had precise figures at his fingertips (after all, they would have been easily obtained by the programme researchers) as well as persuasive reasons for spending so much.

So let's see if we can do a little better ...

*Bill* (after 'intro' to camera): Mr Stuch, why have you not withdrawn your drug from the market?

*Ron*: Because at the moment all the medical evidence we have at our disposal shows there is no connection between Globomin and health problems which have been highlighted in the papers. We are not prepared to deprive tens of thousands of arthritis sufferers of the great blessings of this drug merely on the basis of newspaper gossip. However, we are now putting massive resources into investigating every case of so-called 'side-effects' to establish that there is no connection and that Globomin is as safe as a full programme of testing showed it to be before it was licensed for prescription in Britain.

*Bill*: But if you were to find a connection, would you withdraw the drug?

*Ron*: Yes. Categorically, yes! But I don't believe any connection will be found. Remember, we invested millions in researching and developing this drug to ensure not just its efficiency but – more importantly – its safety. And we have spent more huge sums on informing GPs about Globomin as a treatment for arthritis and related diseases.

*Bill*: Talking about promotion, you're reported to have had a budget of . . .

*Ron*: Two million pounds! Yes, that's another example of our faith in this drug and our concern that the medical profession should be fully briefed about its proper use in treating their patients.

That's better! If you compare the two versions of this interview, you'll note that the real difference is not so much in the facts as in the presentation of the facts.

One more aspect of the controversial or 'hard' interview is that it can often be the easiest to cope with. Tough, uncompromising questions call for straight, uncomplicated answers. Simple!

Problems arise when the interviewee suspiciously looks for hidden meanings and insinuations in questions. That can cause all sorts of trouble. Strangely enough, interviewees ('victims', they like to call themselves) very commonly talk themselves into damaging situations. They not only look for the hidden dagger, they also develop anxiety about tricky questions which might be asked. Then they bring up the difficult issue of their own volition – introducing something that had never been in the interviewer's mind!

A silly example will illustrate what I mean:

## MORE PRACTICE ...

*Question*: Did you beat your wife last night?

The true answer is 'no', but our interviewee is just as likely to answer: 'No, but when I did raise a hand to her last year, it was because ...' and there follows a confession of something quite unknown to the interviewer. Ask any professionals who've been in the reporting business for more than a month or so and they'll confirm that this apparent compulsion to 'confess' is quite common.

Why? I'd need a psychiatrist to explain it properly. All I do know is that it won't happen to you if you're properly trained and approach every interview in a positive spirit.

Yes, we're back to *attitude* again!

CHAPTER EIGHTEEN
. . . . . . . . . . . . . . . . .

# All together now ... the challenges of discussions and confrontations

Most of the media opportunities we've considered so far have assumed a one-to-one interview situation, but there may be many times when the call comes to debate an issue with an 'opponent' or perhaps a number of people in a programme.

All the rules we've laid down – and all the opportunities, too – remain valid, with a few more to be borne in mind.

Let's assume you are asked to appear in a television studio to debate a minimum wage in industry. Your view as a company director is that it's a mistake. You are told that in the studio with you – as well as our presenter, Bill – will be a Mary Smith who is well known for her campaigning to secure the minimum wage.

How do you prepare for this? To begin with, you obtain all the facts you can about Ms Smith, including all the press cuttings and other records there may be of her arguments on the subject. (You may be able to persuade a newspaper, or the broadcaster, to let you see their files.) Make a list of the points she is likely to raise and then marshal your own answers to them. It's the same process as anticipating an interviewer's questions, which I've explained already. Then (and this is important because it's the positive element of your contribution) note down your own most telling arguments against the wage policy. Discuss ideas with your colleagues. Think about them whenever you have a spare moment – in the bath, perhaps, or driving the car.

It's also important to find out as much as you can from the broadcaster about the way the item will be structured and what might be called the 'rules of the game': will Ms Smith be the only other participant? Will the programme be live or recorded? Will there be a studio audience? What will be the duration of the discussion? Who'll be given the first and last word? And so on.

If you're not satisfied with what you're told on these points, fight your corner beforehand, not on air! You may try to make conditions of your own. There's been a growing tendency in recent years, for example, for government ministers to refuse face-to-face arguments with their opposite numbers in the shadow Cabinet. They insist on being interviewed quite separately and (sadly, in my view) the broadcasters usually accept such a condition.

If the intention is to record the programme, then make absolutely sure that your opponent is with you and that the debate really is a debate rather than a series of comments recorded separately and then edited together ('intercut' is the usual phrase). I mentioned the dangers of editing earlier when discussing recorded interviews 'on location'. The dangers of intercutting are even greater and as a rule I would advise you to decline to take part in such an exercise.

You want to try to ensure fair play, too, so seek some assurance that you will both be given roughly equal time (depending, of course, on your ability to justify it!).

When the item takes place, it's more important than ever to listen, not just to Bill's questions which determine the shape of the discussion, but also to Ms Smith's argument. It's devilishly easy to be so wrapped up in your own thoughts about what you're going to say that you fail to hear what she is saying – or, worse still, you *assume* that she has advanced a case with a familiar argument when in fact you haven't taken in her different and unexpected approach. Your riposte to what she has not said will sound, at best, somewhat irrelevant!

You may find that Ms Smith gets under your skin. She may phrase arguments in a way that you find personally insulting. She may try to be a bully and constantly interrupt so that you can

## THE CHALLENGES OF DISCUSSIONS AND CONFRONTATIONS

never complete what you want to say. She may even shout and hog the 'platform' to such a degree that you can't get a word in edgewise. In such a situation, don't try to shout louder and, above all, never lose your temper. If you are seen by the audience to be 'that nice gentleman' who isn't being allowed to state his case, you may win most people's support almost without opening your mouth! And certainly Bill the presenter (with the director in the studio gallery shouting through his earpiece to 'shut that woman up' or something of the sort) will make sure that you have the last word, to try to restore some balance to the argument.

There's a kind of wall-to-wall television style that seems to fill much of our daytime viewing these days – the 'audience participation show'. Usually, there are one or two special guests planted in strategic positions among the audience. It's all very relaxed – dangerously so, if you're one of those guests, perhaps representing your company! The danger lies in forgetting, because of the apparently informal environment, that you need to work just as hard at all the rules of exploiting media opportunities that we've discussed in previous pages. Never be off your guard: directors have a habit of 'catching out' individuals in the audience (it might be you) who metaphorically pick their noses when they think the cameras are focusing on other people who may be speaking in the studio!

And don't try to be too clever. As you become more familiar with the techniques of programme production you'll know that the camera with its red light illuminated is the one whose picture is being transmitted. No, let me rephrase that. You'll *think* you know ... In fact, there are several reasons (which we don't need to go into here) why that might not be the case, so don't relax your vigilance when you think you're 'out of shot'! The best approach is to ignore the cameras, microphones and other moving technology altogether, concentrating exclusively on your (positive) contribution to the programme.

It's always important, but particularly in this kind of show, to remember that we don't all have the same lifestyle and we can alienate many viewers or listeners if we ignore this apparent platitude. Recalling once again my days as *Nationwide* presenter, I used to protest at some of the production team who would draft a scripted link into a studio item with phrases like 'when you took the car out this morning ...' or 'when you finished work this evening ...' The thing they were forgetting, of course, was that a huge proportion of our viewers couldn't afford to own a car or, sadly, didn't have a job. Similarly, if you're a senior businessperson, you won't win many friends (or customers, remember) by referring patronisingly to 'working people' or in some similar way emphasising a divide between you and them.

Avoid, too, the anecdote! Especially in the amiable atmosphere of the audience show, there may be a temptation to 'tell a story' to illustrate a point you want to make. The trouble is, most stories take longer than you think in the telling – certainly longer than the seconds-sensitive TV or radio disciplines can often absorb. So the awful moment comes when, within a sentence or two of your story's crucial punchline, the presenter has to cut you off with a cheerful 'that's all we have time for'.

While we're considering some of the perils of the broadcast media (a negative attitude, I know, but avoiding them enables us to concentrate on the positive) here's one which applies to any kind of show: answering a question by saying something like, 'There are three issues to bear in mind,' and then beginning to enumerate them on your fingers. That may seem a perfectly innocuous way to begin – but it's a recipe for disaster. The likelihood is that you will talk about only two issues. The interviewer will ask: 'What was the third?' And you will have forgotten. (The more I write about lessons of media practice in this book, the more ludicrously simple do some of my examples sound. But I promise you that it's the simplest errors that cause the greatest aggravation!)

One of the unfortunate elements of the audience show is the strong possibility that you are asked to participate – and then never given the chance to say a thing. This may leave you with the angry impression that you have been cheated. ('They put me in the show on the pretext that I'd be able to state my case, but they had no intention of using me.') In fact, your unwilling silence will have a much simpler explanation. In all the years I presented programmes of this kind (like *Talkback*) I could never persuade producers to indulge in simple arithmetic. We'd have, say, a half-hour show and they'd worry that we might fail to fill the time if guests were not very talkative. Forty people might be booked, each expecting to make a contribution. The actual programme time would be 29 minutes, less a minute for titles and credits, making 28. The presenter would need five minutes for introduction, questions and summing-up at the end. That leaves 23. Divide by 40 ... But somehow producers (who can be just as anxious as participants!) could never accept that we had too many guests. They'd always want more, as an insurance against the show running out of steam. Hence the number of aggrieved and thwarted guests who went home believing they were the victims of the broadcasters' manipulation when the real cause was far less sophisticated.

# CHAPTER NINETEEN

## The cosmetics ... putting the gloss on the right foundation

I have deliberately left what might be called media cosmetics to this late stage in the book because it's important to get the *attitude* right first along with the *listening* and, of course, the *content* of any presentation or interview. (It goes without saying that empty waffle can never be a substitute for genuine substance. Press journalists and broadcasters will expose it ruthlessly.)

However, I don't want to give the impression that the 'cosmetics' – perhaps a pejorative term – are of little consequence. Once the basics have been mastered, the personal image can make a crucial difference to selling the message.

A highly-respected consultant in this field is Patricia Frost, who makes large claims about the value of her techniques of presentation and image projection. She says: 'The way you look, move and use your voice account for over 90 per cent of how people perceive you and remember you.' She believes – and I go along with this – that body language is an essential part of the business of communication and if we don't observe its proper practice, messages will become confused and even conflicting. To use the simplest of examples, if you tell an interviewer that your company is prospering – and sit with drooping shoulders, eyes averted – the message will be very different from the words coming from your mouth!

We have discussed already the importance of this kind of body language, eye contact, the warmth of a smile and other fundamental aspects of personal image. Now a word or two about 'superficial' aids which are nevertheless important.

First, dress. This used to be a fairly simple matter. A businessman on a current affairs or business programme knew exactly what to wear: smart dark suit, collar and tie – the 'uniform' of any well-dressed executive. But that's not so any more! (When did you last see the rich and powerful Richard Branson in formal attire?)

Increasingly, the American custom of 'dressing down' in smart casual clothes on a Friday is becoming common practice in business here – even in the pinstriped corridors of City offices. In some of the newer industries and professions, casual wear (even sloppy T-shirts) is worn all the time by some executives. So the choice of clothing for men in a TV or radio studio or a press conference is becoming more difficult. However, there's no question that it's necessary to be smart!

For women, there's a rather different emphasis on choice. To be smart remains a priority, but there are other factors to consider. It's very common in a TV studio or on location, for instance, for interviewees to be asked to wear a radio microphone. This means a little mic clipped to shirt or lapel, with wires attached to a battery, which of course needs to be concealed. For men, that's normally a simple matter. The battery fits snugly into a back pocket. But if a woman is wearing, say, a thin dress, there's a problem! The best that can be done is to put the battery on a strap round the waist and 'hide' it on her back – though, of course, it won't be hidden if she turns round! So I'd normally advise a jacket – with either skirt or trousers.

But what skirt length? Not too short, please! And the neckline of the top shouldn't be too low, either. The obvious reason is that clothes which are especially revealing will distract at least half the viewers. You don't want the male audience more conscious of your legs than of your argument ...

Make-up patently holds no terrors for women, whose personal preferences (little or lots of lipstick, for instance) will be respected by the professionals in the studio make-up room. But men seem to find it an embarrassment. Time and time again I've watched interviewees reluctantly sitting in a chair in front of a mirror,

## THE COSMETICS ... PUTTING THE GLOSS ON THE RIGHT FOUNDATION

protesting: 'I don't usually use make-up.' There really is no need to be embarrassed: a dab of powder, and maybe an application of eyebrow pencil if you're fair-haired, is neither effeminate nor indicative of your sexual persuasion! It's simply a way of making sure you look better through the 'eye' of a camera, and preventing glare from a forehead which may begin to perspire under the heat of studio lights.

All of which is important, because knowing that you look good on screen is a tremendous boost to your confidence – an essential element in a good performance.

Any aid, however slight, to boosting that confidence should be used. When I'm on air and sitting behind a desk, I like to feel 'on top of the job' in the sense of being able to lean down on the desk. So if the chair is too low for my liking, I call for a cushion (or a couple of telephone directories!). I also feel more at ease with a pen in my hand – not to fiddle with, which would become an irritant to viewers, but as a sort of comforter. Or maybe it has become a superstition. No matter. It helps, so I make sure I have it.

When you ask for some aid, however odd it may be, you will certainly not attract the derision of the studio crew. On the contrary, they'll respect your professionalism. Their specific role is to help you to be confident, relaxed and generally at your best.

If you're recording an interview on film or tape out of doors, make sure you're dressed warmly and comfortably (as well as smartly). If you stand shivering in a cold wind, you will certainly not look your best.

There is an awesome list of things that can go wrong when you're recording an interview, especially 'out in the field'. One of the most irritating, in my view, is the kind of day when the sun keeps popping in and out of scudding clouds. Again and again, a 'take' will be abandoned because the camera exposure is ruined by alternate bright light and dark shadow. So the interview has to be interrupted and restarted several times. Now this may be a real challenge to you: it's likely to increase your nervousness; it makes it much more difficult to stay fresh and pretend to be surprised by a question which may have been put to you several times already; and you may begin to think it's your fault that the interview has to be re-recorded, so your confidence is further dented.

MAKING THE MOST OF THE MEDIA

The camera may jam. The battery for your microphone may fail. A gust of wind may cause a noise like an explosion. The tape may run out ... Whatever happens, you must keep your composure and work as intensely at your performance techniques the umpteenth time around as you did at the beginning!

In a radio studio, nerves may lead you to tap on the table in front of you or to tap your feet against the table legs. This will sound more like bombs going off and you'll have to start again!

Timing is all-important but not easy for the beginner. (The pro over the years develops a kind of clock in the brain, becoming highly skilled at 'feeling' the seconds ticking away.) Before any interview, always ask how many minutes – or seconds! – you have available. Then tailor your words to fit, so that you can be sure you have time to include the key message that's going to make it a profitable exercise. There really is no alternative to frequent practice if you're to develop this skill.

Oddly enough, the art of condensing the message into a 'sound-bite' needs to be acquired for talking to the press, too. Provide a reporter with a few well-honed words and they're more likely to be published the way you want than talking at length with the result that a phrase or two not of your choosing will be published.

Before an interview is recorded – or transmitted 'live' – you will probably be asked: 'What did you have for breakfast this morning?' No, the interviewer is not embarking on an embarrassing personal exposé of your lifestyle! He's actually helping the sound recordist to check the 'level' of your voice, and that has become the traditional question to prompt you to say something! Obviously it's helpful if you answer at the same volume level as you're going to use for the real thing. But don't worry too much about that: you'll probably find that nerves make a difference once you're 'under way' and the sound recordist is expert in varying his recording levels to suit. However, if you try to maintain a consistent volume, you'll be his friend for life!

Try to persuade the studio team to seat you so that your 'good side' is favoured by the cameras. You may be perfectly proportioned – in which case, of course, that doesn't matter! – but there may be factors like better hearing in one ear which are all part of the process of being more comfortable and confident.

## THE COSMETICS ... PUTTING THE GLOSS ON THE RIGHT FOUNDATION

How should you address the interviewer – formally or by first name? There's no firm answer to that question. My own view is that you should 'do what comes naturally'. That will come across best to the viewer who's quick to detect insincerity. To address interviewers as 'Bill' or 'Mary' when it's perfectly plain you've never clapped eyes on them before strikes a false note which affects the reception of everything else you say. On the other hand, there's a category of 'friend' which you may never have met but will want to address familiarly. I can't see anybody wanting to call Terry Wogan anything other than 'Terry'. If you did address him as 'Mr Wogan', I suspect he'd take the mickey!

When you receive that call to be interviewed 'live' by telephone, remember that the sound quality will be inferior so there's an extra need for you to speak clearly – and for other sounds (especially a radio in the room) to be eliminated if possible.

For interviews on location, there is normally only one camera available to the director. This means that for close-up shots he can only train it on one face at a time. Normally that face will be yours! But after the interview has been recorded, he will want to take more shots – of the interviewer in close-up and of the two of you together. He will even tell the interviewer to ask his questions all over again without wanting any answers from you. All this palaver is for two reasons: first, the edited tape should look as varied and interesting visually as a studio interview using, say, three cameras. Second, the director needs the extra shots to enable him to edit the tape. For radio, a sound tape can simply be cut up to excise unwanted or 'fluffed' sections, with the ends of tape literally being stuck together with Sellotape – or by the more sophisticated digital methods now more commonly used. But you can't do simple cuts like that in television. Taking a sentence out of the middle of a speech would mean that visually the speaker's head would 'jump' on the screen. To avoid that, the editor 'papers over the crack' by inserting a shot of the listener/interviewer. It's known in the business as a 'noddy' and I only tell you about it because, as elsewhere in this book, I think you are likely to be more comfortable and therefore more adroit if you know the reason for some of the media's apparently strange practices!

As I said at the beginning of this chapter, my shopping list (you may call it a rag bag) of cosmetic skills is less important than the fundamentals we've reviewed earlier. So let me remind you what those fundamentals are, in a very few words:

Develop a positive attitude to the media.
Persuade, project, promote.
Listen and learn.
Watch your language and simplify.
Be prepared.

## CHAPTER TWENTY

# The politicians' way ... and some lessons for businesspeople

The first time I interviewed Margaret (now Baroness) Thatcher, she was Minister for Education and on the first rungs of her ladder to the very top. I remember little of the interview itself, but what followed in the hospitality room afterwards has remained for me a prime example of politicians' appreciation of the part the media plays in their career prospects – and a lesson that businesspeople would do well to heed, if not with quite the same degree of single-mindedness.

She was accompanied by Gordon Reece, her 'minder' who was mostly responsible for her grooming as a communicator through the media. From her commodious handbag she produced a reporter's notebook and began asking me a series of questions about her interview:

Does this suit's shade of blue come over well under the studio lights?

Is my jewellery suitable?

Should I wear a hat?

Was my answer to your questions about free school milk too long?

And so on. Each answer I gave (apolitically, you may be sure!) was painstakingly written down and would no doubt be discussed later. For the many years of political prominence that followed, Margaret Thatcher's attention to the smallest details of appearance and performance never wavered. I didn't always agree with some of the advice she followed – like the softening of her voice which was clearly intended to reduce her early stridency and convey a gentler, warmer, more caring personality. It seemed to me to convey a degree of artistry which eroded credibility. But that is only a personal opinion: the fact is that her dedication and application to making the most of the media was a key factor in her vote-catching success.

Business executives can learn a lot from politicians on this score. In other respects, some of the lessons may be negative ones: above all, the kind of evasion that most politicians practise should be anathema in the commercial and financial world. You know the sort of thing.

'Minister, unemployment figures have reached a new high. What action do you propose to take?'

'Before I answer that, Michael, let me tell you about some fresh statistics showing good progress in the house-building programme ...'

It would be good to think that such blatant evasion and attempted manipulation would get short shrift from interviewer and audience alike. But the game of media politics is not like that. For a start, the audience is as biased as the politician. (There is, in my experience, no such thing as an unbiased viewer.) So the interviewer is on a hiding to nothing.

In the example above, I have two choices. One is to interrupt immediately and insist: 'No, Minister, I want you to answer my question about unemployment.' In that case, roughly half the audience write angrily to the BBC or ITV to protest about my rudeness and arrogant way of refusing to let a minister make his point.

Alternatively, I can give way and provide a platform for the minister's 'party political'. In that event, the other half of the audience complain to the broadcasting authorities that I have shown my own political bias by allowing the minister to exploit the interview.

But the business executive doesn't have any of the audience on his side. If he evades the question or attempts some blatant and unjustified sales line, they're all against him (quite rightly, I have to say!).

It has long been a wild dream of mine that one of the main political parties will enter a general election campaign with a clear edict to all its candidates: 'When talking to the media, always answer the question – and tell the truth.' That is certainly my message to business executives throughout this book, but I fear it will never come to pass in politics. Am I really stupidly naive in thinking that the electors would rally to the party which followed this path? We shall never know the answer to that.

The extent to which political interviewing is a kind of word game is probably not appreciated by most people, however cynical they may be. At first when I joined the ranks of TV and radio current affairs interviewers, I was shocked. I remember vividly one night covering a by-election result. The three combatants in the studio fought a passionate war of words with the government spokesman (whose party's candidate had been defeated). He was torn apart by his exultant opponents who came out with all the usual lines about 'no moral right to stay in power' and 'given notice to quit by a country sick to death of your economic mishandling'. The temperature in the studio rose to boiling point and it was all I could do, it seemed, to maintain a semblance of order and prevent physical blows.

Then it was time to close the programme. The three participants were led down to the hospitality room. The wine was uncorked and the cigars passed around ... and in an atmosphere of complete *bonhomie* an animated discussion ensued between three good friends. The shadow front bencher actually said to the minister whom he'd savaged on air: 'You didn't deserve tonight's result. I think your current stance on the economy is eminently sound.' I couldn't believe what I was hearing. How could responsible Members of Parliament, one of them Her Majesty's minister of state, play intellectual games like that, creating phoney conflict where none really existed, when the future of the country was at stake? No, that wasn't the real question. The real question was: how could I be so naive and unworldly as to believe that political argument through the media was anything other than a knockabout game Westminster people play?

(Incidentally, you may wonder why I have been so coy about naming names in some of my anecdotes. The reason is that there is a tradition, never in my experience broken, that off-the-record conversation in the hospitality rooms – sometimes called 'green rooms' – of television and radio studios are treated with total confidentiality. Politicians feel free to speak with sometimes mind-blowing frankness and honesty, confident that their remarks will never be repeated publicly. The equivalent in the newspaper world, I suppose, is the private lunch – though the reliance on confidentiality may be less assured.)

Nevertheless, my own attitude to 'the game' never became cynical enough to accept it easily, even after many years of being deeply involved in it. Always in my mind has been the recollection of an evening on *Nationwide* during the Heath government's crisis days of shorter working weeks and pay restraint.

In the studio with me was Jack Jones, then general secretary of the Transport and General Workers' Union and one of a powerful group of trade union leaders who wielded immense power at the time. We embarked on a furiously animated discussion about the issue. The cut and thrust became what we'd call 'great television' as we were both in good form that night and my devil's-advocate questions were met with the sharpest of responses. Several minutes into this confrontation, I smiled and said: 'You're enjoying this, aren't you?'

It was one of the silliest things I ever said on air. I regretted it instantly and – not for the first time in a 'live' transmission – wished I could have taken it back. It embarrasses me still. I blush to think that there were something like ten million people watching us. A great proportion of them were working people suffering hardship as they tried to earn enough to pay the rent and feed the family despite inflation that was outpacing their wages. There was a dire prospect that their plight would be worsened by decisions about to be taken by government or unions ... and here was I turning this great human issue into a jolly duel of words!

Among the lessons I learned from that shameful moment was one that applies to us all – and to businesspeople in particular:

always keep in mind the nature of your audience. If you're to get your message across with the best possible impact, don't try to impress your colleagues or the professional interviewer. If you do, you'll almost certainly find yourself on the wrong wavelength as far as your listeners, viewers and readers are concerned. Your language should be in *their* idiom. That's why it is so important before starting an interview to establish whom you're really addressing. There will, of course, be huge differences between programmes or journals which target young or old, consumers, office or factory workers, management, arts or sports lovers and so on. The people who tune in to early evening magazine programmes on television are for the most part very different from those who are regular late-night current affairs addicts. And you must recognise that.

Try to personalise your contribution with references that may strike chords with those audiences. Talk about your family on the early evening show – or about your accountant on *The Money Programme*. Most politicians practise this well and understand its effectiveness. Kissing babies on the election trail may be corny – but it works!

So although there are fundamental differences between the political and the business-orientated interview techniques, there are common basic lessons to be learned.

However, it must be said again that the responsibility for effective and responsible interviewing in the media is not the sole responsibility of the interviewee. Indeed there has been growing concern in recent times about the standards and ethics of the broadcasters themselves. The business magnate Lord Hanson has written (in the *Spectator*) about the de-merits of what he regards as destructive journalism which 'fosters the belief that politicians routinely evade the truth and break their promises ... Business-people, too, are disbelieved; they are castigated for seeking profit, damaging the environment and much else besides. These are easy and emotional targets, making for dramatic television.'

Much of this, according to Lord Hanson, 'reflects not so much maturity and worldly wisdom on the part of the media reporters, as an immaturity deriving from their never having had to do anything in the real world.'

Ouch! That last comment seems to me to reflect the very cheap cynicism of which he complains. There is no doubt that some of his criticism is valid, but it must be said that I sometimes wonder whether businesspeople themselves always live and work in what he calls 'the real world'.

In my view, politicians, businesspeople and media professionals need each other. It is, for example, easy for us all to be snide about politicians – yet the fact is that many of the biggest strides made in commercial and industrial management have been initiated not by businesses but by politicians. As we've already seen, it was the government-inspired Bullock Report which brought about the much-needed revolution in information-sharing in British industry. It was politicians who showed the way in so many fields involving equality of opportunity at work, environmental care and so on (all ultimately profitable developments!).

The relationship between the media people and business is the underlying theme of this book and it's time we took a look at some of the moral arguments about that relationship ...

# CHAPTER TWENTY-ONE

## Being prepared ... the morality of media training through other eyes

I took part in a BBC radio programme (*Medium Wave*) in 1996 that might have been designed to give me apoplexy. In fact, I had to use a large amount of self-discipline to obey the rule I give to others in my training sessions: 'Never lose your temper!'

The subject was media training and it included recorded contributions from two respected media professionals – Roger Mosey, the editor of Radio 4's *Today* programme and Jeremy Paxman, the presenter ('interrogator' might be a better word) of *Newsnight* on BBC2. Both programmes are noted for incisive and intelligent interviewing.

This is how Jeremy's piece began:

> I hate the idea of media training for one overriding reason, and it is that those people who can afford to pay the very extravagant fees charged for media training are those people for whom it is least necessary. And the people for whom it is most necessary can't afford to be trained. The whole point about media training – as it applies to spokesmen for powerful vested interests – is to enable them to put one over on the public in the most plausible manner.

Codswallop! The comment that most angered me in that outburst (though it was gently expressed) was the use of phrases like 'putting one over' and 'plausible manner'. I was genuinely shocked that a responsible interviewer should have that attitude to people who have a view to express – however that view might differ from his own or that of his producer.

People with so-called 'vested interests' are in fact simply people with a point of view or perhaps a political or commercial interest. That's the very reason why they're asked to take part in programmes, so what is the objection to their defending or promoting their interests (not 'vested', please!) in a persuasive and articulate way?

And what's all that about 'extravagant fees'. A typical training session (at least as far as my own company is concerned) is about £1350 for up to five people. In other words, less than £300 per person for a reputed professional trainer, camera, lights and sound equipment, operator, tape, location and so on. I cannot believe that anyone would regard that as 'extravagant' – particularly in relation to what's at stake in many cases (see Chapter 11 on crisis management) or the inestimable value of promotion. Some broadcasters, it seems, regard profit and company promotion as in some way to be despised. Will someone tell me why? Are those of us in business supposed to strive to make a loss?

Roger was much more reasonable – in my opinion! He said:

> If media training is simply a way of getting people to marshal the 400 thoughts they've got in their heads and come up with their thoughts in a clearer order, that's not in itself a bad thing. I think if media training is designed to obstruct interviewers, obstruct the truth and to hide facts – in that case, it is a bad thing.

I have no quarrel with that view – though it has to be said that I have never come across a media training programme (even a third-rate one) that sets out to help people obstruct the truth.

But there was worse to come from Jeremy ...

> Media training is something that people who work as journalists or in the media should not do ... because what they're essentially engaged in is teaching people, who ought to be held to account by the media, to find ways of addressing the issue.

## THE MORALITY OF MEDIA TRAINING

> And so it's an exercise, basically, in dressing up mendacity. On a couple of occasions I did it myself in the past and I felt rather uncomfortable and rather tainted by it and I knew then that I shouldn't do it.

My pulse rate was speeding up as I listened to all that, and my anger was growing when Jeremy concluded:

> To say that media training is essentially about teaching people how to lie persuasively would be to exaggerate what it's all about. That would be to exaggerate the importance of media training and media trainers, but it's not far off the truth.

I was appalled – and made that plain in the programme (which was what the Americans tend to call a 'live recording', in other words a recorded programme which the producer intends not to edit). All this claptrap about teaching people to evade questions! In my training sessions, I do exactly the opposite. My first injunction – as we have seen in the 'checklist' featured in an earlier chapter – is: tell the truth.

Warming to my subject, I went on:

> I'm very concerned about their attitude to the game. What does [Jeremy] think he's about? Does he think he's successful if he brings people into the studio and has them leaving on their knees as gibbering wrecks?
>
> What is his job about? It's about educating, informing and entertaining – the three BBC principles. And he, like the rest of the broadcasters, ought to be particularly grateful to people like us for helping to create articulate, honest people in the studio ... One of the key points I make to people is: you must answer the question. You must not evade it.

There is always a point in an argument of this kind when some confusion arises about the facts. It has to be said that there are some bad trainers around – and some who persuade business-people to pay 'extravagant' fees, for what is the wrong advice. But I was not happy about Jeremy and Roger tarring the rest of us (the majority, surely?) with that particular brush.

## MAKING THE MOST OF THE MEDIA

Less heated, as our radio debate continued, was the question of presenters being 'compromised' by offering their services as trainers – and then possibly facing their pupils on air in what ought to be a balanced, disinterested, even probing way. Nick Gowing, presenter of the BBC's World Service television news, said he had actually 'resisted approaches' to train people. 'I made a decision in my own mind that I did not want to cross the line ... In my view it does compromise a lot of journalists who are asking questions of people whom they are also training behind the scenes.'

It's an understandable – and patently honest – position to take. However, I believe the BBC rule that 'presenters cannot train people' (at least, that's how the rule was described in this programme) is unnecessarily draconian. In my own time under contract to the corporation, I carried out some training which in my own estimation could not possibly lead to a compromising situation. In other words, I was employed to help somebody get rid of nervousness in a studio, fear of a camera or microphone with no political or ethical overtones. If there was any doubt in my mind at all, I would consult a senior BBC executive of impeccable integrity. If he saw potential problems, I would have no hesitation in rejecting a commission – however extravagant the fee!

Is it silly to expect that professionals like me are trustworthy to that extent? Please God, no!

As for the potential client, he is surely right in believing that to learn the art of making the most of the media is every bit as important – indeed, essential – to good business as learning at school to read and write.

## CHAPTER TWENTY-TWO

# In praise of brevity ... and the PR skills that aid communication

I have always liked the little story of the man who wrote a long letter to his friend and concluded with the words: 'I'm sorry this has been such a long letter but I haven't had time to write a short one.'

It teaches that most important lesson – that brevity in writing (as in speaking) is an art not easily acquired, and that it is greatly to be desired as an aid to better communication. Don't ever describe a brief piece of writing as lazy. If it conveys a message clearly and succinctly it may be the fruit of professional hard graft. It may reflect the skills of which the best public relations practitioners are made.

I want to develop the theme of PR influence on the media here, but first let me stay with the merits of brevity by telling of a recent experience of my own with a progressive company in the computer software industry which employed very clever (and mostly very young!) people with a strong line in jargon. After one training session in which I'd extolled the merits of simplicity in communication, I was approached by the marketing manager who told me he was engaged on an exercise to 'clarify the image' of the company. He was working on a memo to distribute to senior staff, explaining the importance of this image among customers and in the media. When he'd completed the memo, could he 'pass it across' me (I think he meant show it to me) for my observations.

## MAKING THE MOST OF THE MEDIA

The memo duly arrived and it was pretty clear to me that the marketing manager was rather proud of it – not least because it was so long (or, in his view, 'comprehensive'). It was, indeed, 28 single-spaced pages of A4. I began to wade through it, slowly sinking in a sea of computer gobbledegook.

Later, I talked to my client on the phone.

'What did you think of my draft memo?' he asked with an unmistakable note of pride in his voice.

I tried to be gentle. 'Well it seems to me that what you're trying to say is encapsulated in the second sentence on page 2 and the first paragraph on page 18. I suggest you need to try to describe the desired image of the company in no more than 50 words. I'll have a go for you if you like.'

'You are a wag,' he said, clearly thinking that the 50-word challenge was some kind of joke. And then: 'I'll take you up on that.'

'All right,' I said, 'are you commissioning me?'

'What do you mean?'

'Well, I reckon it will take about a fortnight's research and drafting to have those 50 words.'

By this time the poor man was utterly bemused. He couldn't comprehend that producing several thousand words might look like hard work but was in fact easier – and far less effective – than crafting a few succinct sentences.

One of the reasons why PR people are poorly regarded by many is that these kinds of skill are imperfectly understood by businesspeople. Sitting at a desk staring at the ceiling may not look quite as productive and energetic as manually operating a machine on the factory floor – but it may betoken intense concentration on producing creative ideas which may be of real value.

So if you are looking for professional PR help to make the most of the media, look above all else for creative talent – not just in writing but in much else besides.

# IN PRAISE OF BREVITY ...

Rightly or wrongly, PR has a bad name in many companies. It ought to be an important part of the process of building a company's reputation – I'd say an essential part – whether it's of the do-it-yourself variety, with skilled people in your own team, or provided externally by one of the hundreds of consultancies around.

However, there are the types who give PR a bad name and can cost a fortune in wasted fees. I'd put these types into a list of those to avoid.

- *The press release addicts.* These are the 'account executives' (they like that label) who see it as their main role to churn out 'news' hand-outs for the press in particular but often to the broadcasters as well. They see volume as a mark of industry (rather like my 28-page memo man) and expect their client to be greatly impressed by the number that are sent out. 'Hasn't she worked hard?' The quality of writing and the worth of the story told is less regarded. Yet the fact is that a steady stream of releases from one company through its PR consultant will often have the reverse effect of what's intended. In my newspaper days as an editor, I would come to recognise the envelopes through the post which contained hand-outs from one major firm – and throw them unopened into the waste paper basket. That was possibly silly of me, because there might occasionally have been a nugget which could have been developed into a good story for the paper – but I had wasted so much time perusing the cascade of paper that I eventually lost patience. An occasional phone call when there was a genuine story on offer – especially if it were offered exclusively and not splashed around every other news outlet – would have brought the company far more (free) column inches.

- *The Sloane Rangers.* Now this may sound sexist and class-biased, but I do believe that many companies, especially in London and the south of England, are paying high fees for little more than a gaggle of young women – expensively dressed in the Knightsbridge uniform, well bred and well connected socially (though with few contacts in the seats of media power), with private school and possibly finishing school but rarely university education – who are little more than window-dressing for their agencies and their clients. Naive to a degree in the rough world of the media, they are best suited to looking pretty on exhibition stands and playing hostess at promotional freebies. They are an expensive and largely pointless luxury!

- *The lunch-club lizards.* I have to temper my criticism here because there are times when the lunch table can provide genuine business opportunities. When I first ventured out of broadcasting and set up my own company with the need to market our services and court clients, I made a resolution: there will be no cocktail cabinet in my office – and no 'business lunches'. I had a lot to learn! The first lesson came when I needed to arrange a meeting within a few days but had no time available. Every morning and afternoon was busy. I found myself saying to my client on the phone: 'The only chance is if you don't mind working through lunchtime.' I called it that, but really it was my first business lunch! And it was the first of many, which I realised added an extra sector to the working day. It was quickly followed by the working breakfast! It's also true (and noted in a previous chapter) that lunches can be a useful way of developing relationships, especially with media people. However, all that is different from the PR lunch-club lizards who regard eating out (and, especially 'drinking out') in the best restaurants at a leisurely pace ('Must be back in the office by three') as a regular perk. There ought to be a notice above their desks, reminiscent of wartime, reading: 'Is your lunch date really necessary?' And there should be a check made to try to relate promotional value achieved to the cost of the bills incurred. I think it would give many a client indigestion.

Good PR, which earns its keep many times over, calls for training, experience, creative ideas, the ability to earn the trust and respect of people in the media, a journalist's feel for a story – and contacts! That trite old saying about 'not what you know but who you know' may have been invented to describe the kind of influence that successful PR people wield. You simply can't beat the person who has a direct line to the decision-makers in the media – and who will always be listened to.

Effective ideas to promote your message or your product need not, it has to be said, always be original. It never ceases to amaze me, for instance, how often newspapers fall for a trick that's been played countless times for as long as I can remember. It's the 'survey' trick.

Let's say you manufacture or distribute Godiva shampoo. Your PR team make a hundred or so phone calls to householders around the country, telling them you're carrying out a national survey on haircare habits and asking them a dozen or so questions. How often do you wash your hair? Do you use a conditioner each time? How often do you visit a hairdresser? And so on.

Then you produce a report which reveals a 'newsworthy' story. 'Scottish women have the cleanest hair.' Or 'Blondes prefer gentlemen who shampoo daily.' Or something equally ridiculous but attractive to the popular paper headline-writers.

The press release does not mention the shampoo at all – but includes the information that the facts about national hair-washing habits are revealed in 'a nationwide survey commissioned by the Godiva Hair-care Institute' – which guarantees the use of the brand name because the papers need to give the source of the story. Creating an 'institute' or 'information bureau' is a good wheeze.

The papers must know it's all a PR game, but they seem willing to play along if the 'survey' is intriguing enough – and if there's not much else around to fill the Monday newspapers.

One final thought on the public relations business: the other day I heard a PR executive tell her clients during a training session that there really is truth in that other trite saying that 'there's no such thing as bad publicity'. I'm afraid that is far from the truth – unless you have the skills to turn bad news to advantage, in the kind of way recorded in previous chapters.

And for all my cynicism in the last few pages, I do believe that the best PR people can help to provide those skills for you as part of a concerted – and never-ending – policy of building bridges to the media.

## CHAPTER TWENTY-THREE

# Awards spell rewards ... how to get your stall out for pots of media gold

I'm often surprised by companies which don't take the trouble to pursue promotional opportunities through the media – but I'm positively gobsmacked by all those which ignore opportunities that are actually offered to them 'on a plate'.

A recent example – indeed, one which continues as I write this – is the search in the south of England for business excellence which is organised each year by Meridian Broadcasting, with a little help from me. Firms in the area are asked to submit entries for the Meridian Business Award which recognises quality, job security, contribution to the local community, care for the environment, profitability and so on. There's plenty of pre-publicity for the competition and it's made very clear that successful companies who enter will be strongly featured in a highly desirable time slot (after *News At Ten*) through this powerful medium. The potential for free promotion worth tens of thousands of pounds is obvious.

And yet ... many firms in this prosperous area don't bother to enter, while others which do fail to put in the sort of effort which deserves to catch the judges' eyes. It is surely obvious that slap-happy filling-in of the entry form – often in lazy or even indecipherable handwriting! – is no way to set about competing for the glittering prize.

I think it's worth looking at some examples of lost opportunities from my experience over the last few years – because they provide lessons for those who really want to pursue this kind of opportunity (and there are many around the country) provided by the media. Each time, the judges provide me with a short-list of companies which I visit with a film crew. I do my level best to report as favourably as possible, but the onus is obviously on each company to show me the best examples of their activities. They have plenty of notice of our visit – plenty of time to 'get their act together'. And what do I find? I'll spare their blushes by keeping names out of this, but the following cases are entirely authentic.

*Company A* manufactures home DIY materials and submitted an extremely impressive entry, all put together in a well-designed presentation pack. But when we arrived at the main offices to 'shoot' the story – after they had been given a week or so's notice of our intentions – we were faced with a handful of staff who had no idea what was going on. The marketing director thought we might 'talk to one or two of my people'. The managing director asked if we'd like to record a meeting going on in his room. Aghast, I started to ask about all the activities of the company described in the competition entry – and discovered that they bore no relation to the pedestrian facts! Not only that, but the PR agency people who had made the submission were not even present.

*The lesson*: Don't fall into the trap of thinking that glossy PR can open the door to valuable media exposure. If there's no substance behind the promotional claims, you may find your company exposed in a rather different, and seriously damaging, way.

*Company B* thought they were much cleverer and had a shooting schedule all ready for us when we arrived. Their entry had laid special emphasis on investment as part of the company's progressive policies. So we were escorted by the MD to a site which had recently been bought and which would eventually provide valuable room for the company's expansion. The journey called for a precious hour's driving out of an allocated half day's filming, but we were assured it was a key factor in their submission. It turned out to be a totally derelict area of scrubland surrounded by a rusting wire fence.

*The lesson*: You really must give thought to the medium as much as to the message. 'We have invested a million pounds in acquiring new sites to expand production' may sound impressive in print. But a picture of dereliction tells exactly the opposite story! That may seem unfair, but it can't be changed.

*Company C* were equally diligent in setting out their stall for us and arranged a visit to a local school to see voluntary work their staff had done there as part of their claim to be making a significant contribution to the life of the local community. And there was no doubting the validity of the claim. The headmaster was eager to testify to the value of the company volunteers' efforts. There was just one snag – but for filming purposes it was a crucial one. We were taken to the school at four o'clock in the afternoon ... when there wasn't a single pupil and precious few teachers on the premises! Empty classrooms and cavernous corridors do not constitute exciting television.

*The lesson*: Give more thought to the photo opportunities you offer the media. Try to visualise the image you're promoting and choose the best circumstances to photograph, record or write about it. Obviously, that headmaster's testimonial would have had several times the impact if it had been recorded to a bustling background of happy chattering schoolchildren.

*Company D*: Actually there were many examples like this. It is a retail chain and we went to the flagship outlet. That's where the chairman has his office – above the shop. And that was the reason we were asked to go there. The chairman was, it became clear, the beginning and end of the story. *He* would be interviewed. Wasn't that enough? To us, of course, it was far from satisfactory, but no other members of the company team had been lined up for interview and no activities of

## MAKING THE MOST OF THE MEDIA

visual interest were suggested to us. Perhaps it was not surprising that the chairman turned out to be a pompous, self-satisfied bore. And the impression of his company was a reflection of that.

*The lesson*: The media are unmoved by formal status and would far rather talk to the office boy than the chairman, if that's where the 'news angle' is to be found. If you are the chairman, you should turn a deaf ear to the sycophants around you and delegate the role of media spokesperson to someone else on your staff unless you're truly a 'natural' – and have been well trained as well!

There have been so many other examples of opportunities lost by companies since we launched the Meridian Business Awards four years ago: too little time and thought devoted to the entry form and application; a failure to involve employees so that they respond well when the camera crew arrives; too little thought about visual interest; even carelessness over basic health and safety regulations (so that shots of the factory may show damning evidence of carelessness!).

Here are some of the things you should aim for if you want to respond to media offers of publicity:

Make sure you have a sound story to tell.

Prepare employees so that they want to give the best impression.

Select particular employees to be offered as interviewees – and give them professional training.

Choose good visual settings that will reflect your company's excellence.

Offer simple – but greatly appreciated – help to your visitors, like transport, carrying their heavy gear around a factory floor, a room set aside for their use, a cup of coffee ...

Above all, adopt a positive attitude so that they feel your company has pride in what it produces. (No skeletons in *your* cupboards!)

## AWARDS SPELL REWARDS ...

And, afterwards – after all your hard work has brought its deserved reward with the great prize of media exposure – make sure you add value by publicising your success in every other way possible, like the trade press, advertising, direct marketing and all the rest.

There are so many 'business awards' on offer nowadays in all the media that there's bound to be one you can win ... if only you're willing to invest significant and intelligent effort.

What a waste to ignore the opportunity!

## CHAPTER TWENTY-FOUR

# You're on your own ... the individual's guide to fame and fortune

Most of what has been written so far has concerned the promotion of your company through the media. Now let's consider *you*!

After all, doing your best for your company may be your prime objective – but there will be great advantages to you personally at the same time. Certainly a reputation for good performances will count strongly in your favour when the boss is assessing promotion prospects in the management team. It will also catch the eye of other companies and their head-hunters! If you are the chairman or chief executive, then it's the shareholders and investors you'll impress. It could even lead to a whole new career path.

But there may be, in your own perception, personality 'handicaps' which stand in the way of being a good performer.

Like shyness.

Now let me tell you something about shyness. Many, if not most, of the truly star performers I've known in a lifetime in the media are extremely shy people! I won't go as far as to claim that only shy people can succeed in publicity's glare – but they certainly stand a better chance than the outwardly confident extroverts who so often crumble as soon as a camera or a microphone is pointed at them. (It's all very puzzling. A shy person walking into a strange pub, say, may feel mortified and feel the blood rushing to his cheeks. He thinks everyone is looking at him. But why? Doesn't that mean he's an egotist, the apparent opposite of a shy person and self-centred to an inordinate degree? Otherwise why should he consider himself the centre of attention?)

One possible reason for shy peoples' skill as performers is their driving need to overcome their 'affliction'. They make themselves face the spotlight as a kind of therapy.

Or again it may have something to do with audiences being paradoxically a kind of protective cover: strangely, it may be easier to stand in front of a crowd and speak to them than to face a single person eyeball to eyeball in a personal and possibly emotional conversation.

The television camera can become a 'friend' to such people and somehow inspire them to perform well. I know a number of star performers who visibly change when the lights are switched on and the camera rolls. They have, it has been said, a love affair with the piece of hardware.

This is not the same as being 'photogenic', which means that you have a well-shaped face (probably with prominent cheekbones) which, as they say, 'photographs well'. No, I'm referring to that small band of performers who actually seem to change shape when the cameras are on them. I sometimes work with a girl – who had better remain nameless! – who can turn up for work looking, to put it brutally, a mess. Overweight, rather baggy features, sloppily dressed ... I feel like telling her that it's time she 'pulled herself together'. Then the cameras roll – and instantly I watch an attractively warm personality, somehow looking a million dollars and striking up an instant rapport with anybody watching.

So, if you have ambitions to develop your skills on television or radio – or perhaps talking to a 'live' audience in the flesh – don't be deterred by the fact that you're shy or (in your own eyes) lacking in obvious physical glamour. You may well have the magic ingredient that is sometimes called 'star quality'.

At the same time, don't run away with the idea that the quality we're discussing is entirely 'natural', or that there's little you can do to change the way you are if you think you lack that 'magic'.

There are obvious (but often ignored) ways of preparing yourself to face the cameras or the microphones or the journalist's flashbulbs. Make sure you have a good sleep the night before – yes, my advice is as simple as that! Have a long lingering bath and wallow in it as you prepare mentally and emotionally. In the modern jargon I suppose it may be called 'psyching yourself up', but certainly it's an important part of the process. Exercising will help, too. It doesn't need to be anything drastic! Simple muscle-loosening knees-ups and swinging your arms will do. There's no need to be embarrassed about this because it can all be done in the privacy of your own home. The aim is to clear the brain and develop the positive relaxed-but-alert attitude that's going to make the crucial difference between a competent and an outstanding performance.

Am I going over the top? Do you really need to go to such lengths just for a media opportunity? Yes, I think you do – because the stakes may be so high. (I've already told how a one-minute appearance on BBC's *Panorama* became the watershed in my own career. If I had failed to prepare myself thoroughly, the opportunity of a lifetime would probably never have arisen again.)

But you need to do more than prepare for a single performance. Train yourself long-term for all the different situations that may arise. I think that perhaps the most valuable talent of all is to be able to speak without notes – not just because you will certainly perform better looking directly at your audience rather than down at your notes, but also because you will be so much better able to cope with a request without any warning to 'say a few words' on a public occasion, or perhaps to respond to an out-of-the-blue telephoned interview from one of the media.

I was 17 years old when I began regular speaking in public. My audiences then were youth clubs in Glasgow. I was writing a column for young people at the time in the *Sunday Mail* and I was often asked to give talks on subjects like 'a day in the life of a newspaper reporter'. A simple enough task, really, but I deliberately made it harder for myself by resolving never to read a speech – a resolution I have never broken to this day. Arguably my audiences in those days suffered from this and might have heard rather more articulate talks if I had written them down! But I certainly benefited and with hindsight I'm glad of the self-imposed discipline.

We discussed in Chapter 3 the recommended routine of writing down the 'headlines' of an intended speech and then absorbing them mentally in a logical progression so that you will eventually be able to speak to your theme 'from memory'. That does not mean learning a script word for word as actors are required to do. (I don't think Shakespeare ad libbed would go down too well in the RSC.) However, there may be times when one or two key phrases need to be learned and my tip for doing that is to read and re-read the passages, until you have ingested their meaning. Only then do you learn the actual words. You'll find it much easier to remember them; you'll deliver them much more persuasively; and you'll be much more at ease with them so that you're less likely to panic and forget.

The kind of nervousness that stems from lack of preparation and of understanding is the worst kind of threat to learning words or phrases.

The other day I was working as a presenter on a marketing video about healthcare products. One sequence involved interviewing a research scientist about the efficacy of some dressings the company had developed. Naturally (as the intended audience was largely healthcare specialists) there were some key medical or technical phrases that had to be absolutely accurate. In a draft script, they were linked by simple conversational phrases that could be changed to suit the researcher's personal style.

He was a nervous man and the director of the video was worried about him. 'Don't worry,' I said boastfully. 'I'll sort him out.' And I embarked on a little lesson, repeating most of what I've written above. Ready to record, he was happy (relatively, anyway!) and we conducted an interview which was exactly what was needed. He used his own words and repeated from the script only those technical phrases which had to be precise. He was hugely relieved – until the director said we'd need to do it all over again (not uncommon when recording) because of problems with the camera. That was too much for my interviewee. He reached for the script to refresh his memory. I could see he was becoming very nervous and took the script out of his hands, urging him to relax and not worry at all about repeating the same words as in the first 'take' – except for the key medical phrases with which he was perfectly familiar, anyway.

We started recording again – and he stumbled over his words. 'Take three,' called the director.

'Don't worry,' I said. 'Just talk to me in your own style and ignore everything else that's going on around us.' But he kept glancing away at the script that was out of reach, looking increasingly like a drowning man watching a lifeboat drift away.

The third take lasted only a few seconds before he completely dried up and with shaking hands grasped the script. 'I won't read it – just let me have it on the table in front of me and I promise I won't look at it,' he said. And, of course, I knew exactly what would happen.

'Take four.'

The researcher spoke just three words (with total panic in his eyes) and glanced down at the script. He looked up for a moment at me – and then down went the head again. This time, of course, he couldn't find the place in the text . . .

I'm not sure how many takes we recorded that morning, but eventually we had to abandon the interview completely. We almost had to give our researcher some of his company's medical care!

That is not an uncommon story – and it stems quite simply from a reliance on learning written words.

So I repeat: absorb the meaning, not the words!

The more opportunities you get to visit studios or locations and watch the professionals at work, the better. Simply being in a studio audience (you can usually apply for tickets) will give you an invaluable feel for the working environment of a TV or radio programme and will enable you to study the ways in which a presenter or interviewer goes about his job.

Even more useful is to secure an invitation to the control room of a show (especially a 'live' one) which will probably make your mind up for ever that you never want to go near a studio again – or that you're fired up to make a name for yourself.

In my days on *Nationwide* – admittedly an unusually demanding programme, with 11 studios all 'on air' at the same time – I often received letters from people who wanted to develop their communication skills and who asked for advice. I would invite them to watch the show from the control room as it went out and then to have a chat with me afterwards. Many times they would turn up – and then vanish without coming to see me because they found the whole operation terrifying! But others were 'hooked' on what those of us in the business find addictively exciting and stimulating.

In previous chapters I've tried to provide basic tips on performing for the media – but at the end of the day, your ability to make full use of the tips must depend on your personality.

If you *want* to be a star performer as a business spokesperson, you will be!

## CHAPTER TWENTY-FIVE

# Don't take my word for it ... listen to the other professionals!

As I hinted at the very start of this book, one of the serious drawbacks of attempting it is that it seems to reflect a most extraordinary arrogance. Here am I giving lofty advice – which suggests I place myself in the top rank of media practitioners when, in fact, I still have so much to learn. I've even been rude about some people who really are in that top rank!

So let me try to redress the balance in a tiny way by reporting briefly the advice of others – successful professionals in both the production and presentational spheres who have spent years in the business of piloting 'amateurs' through the sometimes rough waters of 'the interview'.

For instance, Robert Rowland. Notable in his long career in television was his editorship of *Panorama*, which many might consider the kind of heavyweight investigative current affairs programme liable to strike terror in the hearts of any business executive called upon to be interviewed for it. Even hardened politicians regard it as a tough challenge. He told me this:

> The most important feature for any executive or employee interviewed about his or her company is to have pride in what the company represents and confidence in the argument which is to be deployed.
>
> If you feel weak on either front, you shouldn't be doing the interview – and perhaps you shouldn't be working for the organisation.

Confidence, and knowledge of your brief, will act as the strongest defence against the most penetrating interview.

This point about 'knowing your brief' is one I've emphasised in different ways throughout this book and it's repeated in a sense by Sue Lawley, my colleague on *Nationwide* for many years but since then admired as an interviewer at many different levels – Desert Island Discs on radio, her own 'talk show' and countless other roles on television. She says:

> Relax and be yourself. It really is as simple as that. Never forget that you know more than the interviewers who are asking the questions!
>
> Provided you have done your homework and got your facts straight, your superior knowledge can enable you to run rings round the most aggressive of interviewers.

Another major name in the television world who has been a star performer for what most people would call a lifetime (though he had two careers as footballer and administrator before being a TV pundit!) is Jimmy Hill. He normally specialises in soccer, of course – but that's an exceedingly commercial activity now involving billions of pounds, so it's very much within the compass of this book. Jimmy says:

> Look the interviewer in the eye and answer the question. You'll certainly know the answer because it will be your subject.
>
> I must admit that nowadays standards of interviewing have slipped in many areas and you should be prepared for difficulties in answering questions because of interviewers' bad techniques.
>
> For instance, you are not helped by the interviewer who, instead of asking a question, makes a statement and asks you to deny it! It drives me round the bend. You may be asked a question which begins something like: 'How pleased were you when ...?' Wait a minute, you may not have been pleased at all, so you can't answer the question as put but need to deny the basic assertion. That makes it very difficult for you. If I'm watching an interview like that, I switch off – but you're stuck

with it and the only advice I can give is not to accept false statements when they're made in the guise of a question.

Stick to the facts – your own facts!

John Morrell is now assistant director of programmes and production at Meridian Broadcasting. His experience of producing hard-hitting and often highly emotive interviews has notably included his years as producer of Esther Rantzen's *That's Life* programmes. He is, at heart, a journalist, which accounts, I suppose, for the simplicity (and wisdom) of his advice:

1. Succinct answers. No waffle.

2. Answer the question that is put – however embarrassing.

3. Demonstrate genuine enthusiasm and commitment.

4. Above all, respect the viewers. They're a bright lot.

I must add my own comment to that last point. Probably the biggest mistake most commonly made by broadcasters is to underestimate the audience. Smart alecs in marketing and advertising keep pushing the programme-makers down market. They clamour for more game shows, soaps and kitchen comedy.

These are supposed to be the fodder of high ratings. Of course there's no denying that they attract millions. But look at the millions who watch classical drama (*Pride and Prejudice* comes to mind) or who switch on to the best current affairs output. *Nationwide* regularly pulled in ten million viewers in the early evening – and in my view its success was largely due to them, not us! A significant proportion of ideas and items stemmed from viewers' own suggestions. And we never patronised them. Nor should you!

Anyway, to some more advice ...

Tim Brooke-Taylor is a wise man of many parts whose skills range over comedy writing and performing in TV's *The Goodies* and radio's *I'm Sorry, I'll Read That Again* to serious presenting of the video library *Career Best* for young people. He's both interviewer and interviewee, so he sees the qualities required from both standpoints:

> I always used to think of an interviewer as the enemy. I felt I was there to be tricked. Today, as an interviewer myself, I bless the subject who treats me as a friend. We are a partnership whose whole purpose is to impart the relevant information. Now when I am being interviewed I try to help, and the good news is that it also helps me.

For my money, Michael Parkinson is one of the most intelligent, sensitive and stylish radio, TV and newspaper interviewers around, and has been for years. In television particularly, his interviews rightly swell the BBC archives and are repeated regularly. What does he look for when people enter the studio to sit opposite him in a long 'in-depth' interview?

> I wait for the moment to occur when I know they're talking to me and not performing for the studio and its surroundings. It's a sea change in the relationship between us and it may take as little as 30 seconds or as long as 15 minutes.
> If it doesn't happen at all, then the true conversational feel of an interview, looking each other straight in the eye, relaxed, revealing, won't be achieved.
> Waiting for this magic moment is something that's happened with everyone I've ever interviewed.

I quoted earlier my first confrontation with Nigel Dempster of the *Daily Mail*, long established as the newspaper world's leading diarist. How does he see the relationship between himself and the typical high society or top business figure he interviews?

> Obviously I hope I'm going to be given the untrammelled truth! But, of course, I'm often frustrated because rich people particularly have a habit of hiding important facts about themselves.
> I understand their fears, of course, and you are right in your book to warn of the dangers of putting too much trust in reporters nowadays, or of relying too easily on an agreement that what the interviewee may say really will be 'off the record'.
> But I still think the businessman and the pressman can achieve what they both want by putting all their cards on the

table in the manner of Tony Wedgwood Benn, who ostentatiously brings out a tape recorder whenever he is interviewed.

That's the best insurance. As the reporter starts to record your conversation, show him your own recording machine. Then we can both aim for what I regard as my target – verité!

Caroline Righton is one of the busiest of today's presenter/interviewers on both radio and television – breakfast-time current affairs, business programmes, satellite news features – the lot! She says:

> I hope people I interview will have learned to be relaxed – and that they'll show their desire to develop a friendly relationship (however grisly the subject of our interview!) when we first meet before going on air. They shouldn't appear intimidated.
>
> I would tell people to remember that messages travel through the eyes. Television can be cruel and the merest flicker of an eyelid can tell the viewer that you don't mean what you're saying.
>
> On the other hand, the right eye signals can express warmth and credibility.

So there you have it – the distilled wisdom of successful professionals who have been producing or practising the art of media interviewing throughout their careers.

Thank goodness they all underline many of the points that I have made: there's no need for me to rewrite the book!

# Index

advertising costs 14
Allied Medical Group (AMG) 94–5
anecdotes, avoid 132
ANRs (audio news releases) 103–4
*Any Questions?* 59–60
appearance, personal 49–50, 50–1, 57, 136–7
attire 49–50, 136
attitude, the right 17, 82, 126–7
audience participation programmes 131–3
audiences
   target 43, 145
   underestimating 171
autoscript systems 87–8

Bishop, Sir Michael 13–14
Blackman, Honor 71–2
body language 23, 54–6, 135
Bowen, Michael 60
brevity, importance of 151
British Midland 13–14
Brooke–Taylor, Tim 171–2
Bullock report (1977) 93, 94
business awards 157, 161

cameras, television 54, 131
Chromakey 50
Co-Operative Society 11–12
commercials, costs 14
communication
   company internal 94–100

importance of simplicity 32, 35–6
and jargon 33–5
written and spoken 32–3, 58, 60
concentration 54, 118
Cook of the Realm 41
crisis management 78–82
Curran, Charles 18

deadlines, newspaper 67–8
debates 129–33
Dempster, Nigel 65–6, 172–3
Dimbleby, Richard 47
discussions 129–33
dress 49–50, 136
Driberg, Tom 18

editing, dangers of 74, 130
education content of interviews 10, 45
Elizabeth (Queen Mother) 37–9
empowerment 99
English, written and spoken 32–3, 58, 60
entertainment content of interviews 10, 45
eyes 52, 173

floor managers 45–6
Frost, Patricia 135

*Gardener's Question Time* 58–9
Gemmell, Alan 58, 59
Gilliat, Sir Martin 38, 39
*Good Life?, The* 95

# INDEX

Griffin, Major John 38, 39
grooming, personal 50–1

hands, what to do with 55
Hanson, Lord 145
headlines, think 68
helplines, training company 113
Hill, Jimmy 67, 170–1
honesty, importance of 65, 96
Hopkins, Mike 79, 81–2

ICI 34–5, 94
image 135
　*see also* personal appearance
influence over the media 37–41
information content of interviews 10, 45, 118
Ingham, Sir Bernard 67
intercutting 130
interviewees 45
　advice from the professionals 169–73
　body language 23, 54–6, 135
　common faults 115–19
　and the first question 52, 53
　and interviewers 10, 18–19, 21, 73, 139
　preparation 26, 49–53, 57, 135–7, 164–5
　and the press 64–5, 68–9
　the right attitude 17–18, 49, 126–7
　in the studio before the interview 45–6, 138–9
　you are the expert 73–4, 170
interviewers 10, 17–18, 145–6
　bad 35, 71–3
　and interviewees 18–19, 21, 73–4, 139, 170–1, 171–3
　preparations 46–7
　techniques 51–2
interviews
　bad 115–19, 123–5
　good 119–21, 125–6
　location 74–5, 139
　off-the-cuff 75
　outdoor 137–8
　press 64–5, 68–9
　radio 57–8, 138
　recorded 74–5
　value of 12–13

ITC (Independent Television Commission) 105

Jaques, Lord 11–12
jargon 33–5
Johnson and Johnson 79
Jones, Jack 144
journalists 63–4, 68
　*see also* interviewers; press, the

Kray, Ronald 19–21

language, use simple 32, 35–6
Lawley, Sue 170
listening skills
　in business 99
　interviews 25–8, 118
　speech-making 28
Loads, Fred 58, 59
location interviews 74–5, 139
lunches 68, 154

magazines *see* press, the
make-up 136–7
manipulation of the media 21, 37
media power 10–16
　negative aspects 21–3
memory lapses 52–3
Meridian Broadcasting 105, 157
Meridian Business Awards 157, 160
Morgan, Dilys 65–6
Morrell, John 171
Mosey, Roger 147, 148

*Nationwide* 11, 40–1
nervousness 53–4, 137, 166
newspapers *see* press, the
'no comment', never say 64, 68–9
Nurse of the Year 40–1

Occidental Oil 80
outdoor interviews 137–8

Parkinson, Michael 172
patronising attitudes 118, 131–2
Paxman, Jeremy 147, 148–9
personal appearance 49–50, 50–1, 57, 136–7
personality 163–4

# INDEX

persuasion 56
phone–ins 61
Piper Alpha oil rig tragedy 79–80
politicians 142, 143–4
posture 54
'PR hour' 39–40
PR people 40, 152–5
presentation, personal 135–6
　　see also personal appearance
presentations 83–4, 85–6, 87–8, 90–1
　　bad 84–5, 86–7, 88–90
presenters see interviewers
press, company internal 96–7
press, the 43, 63
　　negatives of dealing with 64–5, 68–9
　　nurturing good relations with 66–8
product placement 104, 105
programme-making methods 43–7, 139
　　observing 167–8
projection 56, 135
promotion 56, 101
　　helping the media 137–41
　　lost opportunities 105–6, 157–60
　　proactive 40–1, 101–5
　　using opportunities 39, 160–1
　　value of using the media 10–14, 15–16
public speaking 28–9, 165–6
　　see also presentations
pulse rates, presenters' 16

*Queen Mother* 37–9

radio 43, 57–61, 138
　　ANRs 103–4
Reckitt and Colman Pharmaceuticals 40
relaxation 54
reporters see journalists
Reuters Television 102–3
Righton, Caroline 173
Rowland, Robert 169–70

shyness 110, 163–4

simplicity of communication, importance of 32, 35–6
smiles, effect of 55, 57
soundbites 68, 75, 138
Sowerbutts, Bill 58, 59
speech–making 28–9, 165–6
　　see also presentations
spoken and written English 32–3, 58, 60
sponsorship 104
'star quality' 164

target audiences 43, 145
Taylor Woodrow 94
*Team Television* 94
television
　　impact of 12, 14, 15
　　programme–making methods 43–7, 139, 167–8
　　VNRs 101–3
tension, relieving 54
Thames Water 96, 97–8
*Thames Water News* 96
Thatcher, Baroness 141–2
timing 138
training, media
　　getting the best 108–111
　　helplines 113
　　morality of 147–50
　　need for 107
　　sessions 15, 111–13, 115–21
truth
　　cannot be hidden 21, 23
　　tell the 96, 100
Tylenol painkiller 79

video 93–4
　　company internal communications 94–6, 97–9
　　VNRs (video news releases) 101–3
visual aids 83–6

Wheeler, David 32
*Woman's Realm* 41
written and spoken English 32–3, 58, 60

**176**